GOLDEN
NUGGETS

Wisdom from
Above and Below
the Heavens

Dr. Dennis C. Golden

Golden Nuggets
Wisdom from Above and Below the Heavens
by Dr. Dennis C. Golden

Printed in the United States of America.

ISBN 9781498436830

www.xulonpress.com

TABLE OF CONTENTS

Introduction

FULFILLING MY DUTY

"Whoever survives a test, whatever it may be, must tell the story. That is his duty." – Ellie Wiesel

I am a second generation American citizen. My heritage is Irish, Italian, and Russian Jewish. My mother, Marie Rose Kerns, was born in New York City. Her mother, Victoria Toscani, was born in Tuscany, Italy. Her father, Dennis John Kerns, was born in the USA and his parents came from Cork, Ireland. My father, Mayer Golden, was born in New York City, and both his mother, Tilly Furman Golden, and father, Samuel Golden, came from Belarus, Russia. My mom was the second oldest of four children, two boys and two girls. My dad was the oldest of four children. There were three boys and one girl. Mom and dad grew up in the same town where they raised me, Bayside, Queens. However, they came from very different backgrounds. Dad had to grow up very fast and hard. He became a street smart and street tough young man all too early.

I am the only child of Marie and Mayer Golden. I was born in NYC and am now seventy-three years young at the writing of this book and trying to fulfill my duty. As I share these stories, I do so while humbly thanking God for the opportunities and challenges of my life and the lessons learned via my actions both good and bad.

After a forty-eight year career in higher education, I retired in June of 2104. After being all in for decades, I was apprehensive and did not know what to expect. I kept thinking about what people had told me over the years about writing a book about my varied life experiences. After taking this thought to prayer, I decided to do it.

This is not a book about higher education. It is about a Christian under construction, sharing the stories from my youth to adulthood in order to strengthen the reader to face life's situations and set goals for the future. Each story is supported by a scripture passage and a brief Golden Nugget. This format is designed to help the reader think, reflect, and discern in a manner to strengthen ones' faith.

Writing this book proved to be an honest, very challenging and humbling experience, but it was worth the time and effort if just one person is strengthened for his or her life's journey.

Scripture Passage:

Contemplate Ephesians 6:1-4.
What does this say our relationship should be with family members?
Describe your relationship with your parents.
Describe your relationship with your spouse and your children.
According to Ephesians 6:1-4, what things do you need to change in these relationships to obey God?

Golden Nugget:

It is our duty to pass on what we have learned to the next generation. The lessons we have learned are not just for us, we need to use them to help others who come after us.

As you begin your journey through this book, begin to think of how you can fulfill your duty toward using your life experiences to help the next generation.

PASSAGE 1
GROWING UP

NOT A CRADLE CATHOLIC

My parents were not Saturday or Sunday people, so I never experienced a synagogue or church service during my early years. In about the sixth grade, I started playing basketball with two of my friends for a Protestant church. Before traveling to a playoff game, the minister told us he wanted us to arrive early so that we could have our Bible lesson and prayers prior to our departure. This required an earlier dinner, so, I told my mother what the minister had requested. My mom asked me if I liked the Bible lessons and I said, "Yes." She then prepared my early dinner, we had the Bible lessons and prayers, and and then went out and won the game.

The very next day, my mother "got religion" and drove me to the Rectory of Our Lady of the Most Blessed Sacrament Church. She introduced me to Fr. Masterson, and I started my Catholic religious instructions. For the next few years, I took CCD (Confraternity of Christian Doctrine) lessons, and received the Sacraments of Baptism, Holy Communion, and Confirmation.

I also began playing basketball with the CYO (Catholic Youth Organization) team, and we made it to the championship game but lost. Lessons were learned that night and a whole new world started to open up for me. God was giving my mother, father, and me a wakeup call to acknowledge Him, to recognize Him, to pray to Him, to serve Him, and to try to be better through a relationship with Him. God knew the temptations that were ahead for me and knew I needed this time of training and equipping.

My new friends included the younger brothers of some gang members and, as you will read later, their influence had the potential to become a real and present danger. I also met many other new friends with whom I have had lifelong trust and confidence. Additionally, I paid close attention to what the nuns were teaching us in CCD; I started to attend Mass regularly and liked it. During the seventh and eighth grades I felt better about myself. Religious instruction was good for me, I was becoming a different person. I liked the person I was beginning to become.

Scripture Passage:

Explore Acts 9:1-30.

What were some of the key verses for you in this passage of scripture? Write them out and then explain why they were meaningful for you. How can you use them to help others in their life's journey?

Golden Nugget:

I realized that there was another whole culture comprised of priests, nuns, coaches and good people who would willingly help my parents and me. I felt that I belonged to something much bigger than anything I had ever experienced before.

-2-

THE PS 130 EXPERIENCE, SPORTS, AND CAMP

I attended Public School 130 on Francis Lewis Blvd, Bayside, Long Island, NY. I liked going to school because it meant being with my classmates, playing with them in the school yard, and then meeting with them after school. However, I did not really like being in school. I tried to concentrate, but I did not really apply myself. Thus, I was not a good student in elementary school. Many of my grades were C's, D's, and F's. Often the teachers would indicate on my report card that both my grades and behavior needed improvement. Looking back at it, I was on the pathway to becoming a juvenile delinquent.

However, the influence of the CCD classes kept me semi-grounded. Sports activities such as CYO basketball, Little League, the PAL (Police Athletic League), schoolyard football games, and most certainly, the Flushing YMCA began to show me I could do well, at least in sports, if I applied myself.

There was a mixture of race, creed, and color at the YMCA. My involvement there led to great fun, plenty of participation, and about eight summers as a camper, counselor-in-training, junior counselor, and ultimately a counselor at the YMCA Camp Brooklyn in Hawley, PA, with people attending from all areas of metropolitan NYC. The energy and diversity at Camp Brooklyn were incredible; we all loved being out of the city during July and August.

God was letting me know that I was becoming good at sports. He also blessed me with role models and coaches who showed me that we can grow and learn life lessons through sports. Hard work, dedication, fair play, following the rules, the joy of winning, and how to remain a good sport even when we lost were lessons learned as I was drawn into this world of sports.

God was also letting me know that I had a long way to go beyond sports. Listening to the older boys talk about school, I heard about the importance of good grades, and proper behavior. I was waking up to the fact that I needed to change for the better, so I started to think more before speaking and acting. Even though I was learning to work harder, I started to understand that there were much better athletes and much smarter people out there, and competition was going to get increasingly harder. A subtle, but important phase of transformation began as I realized I needed to work more diligently in both school and sports if I wanted to achieve success in my life.

The right people at the right time can make positive, significant, and lasting differences in people's lives. I owe a great debt of gratitude to all of those who helped me along the way. I will never forget their goodness and positive influence, and I have tried to do the same for others over the years.

Scripture Passage:

Softly sing or intone Psalm 16:1-3.

> *Will you pray this as your prayer today?*
> *Will you remain alert to those people God sends across your path to help and guide in His ways?*
> *Will you acknowledge and thank God for His loving care and protection over you?*

Golden Nugget:

Looking back, God was leading me on a connective pathway that would provide for future growth and development. Even though I was young I was beginning to like the changes I could see in myself like making better choices in my friendships, work, and study habits, and in my attitude toward life in general.

-3-

COLLECTING FOR
CEREBRAL PALSY

Although I was growing via my religious instruction and athletic ability, I fell short when it came to personal integrity and activities with some of my friends. As the story goes, one of them had an idea that we could earn some easy money by asking people to contribute to the Cerebral Palsy fund. We rang doorbells and gave our spiels in the apartment houses near PS 130. We collected about $30.00 in two days – easy money. Of course, we were frauds with no affiliation to any Cerebral Palsy fund. My conscience really started to bother me, but I had not yet been "knocked off my high horse."

Then, "on the third day," which I was later to come to understand is an ironic phrase, we started collecting from private homes in our neighborhood. I rang the doorbell, and a very gracious woman opened the door. After I made my false request, she offered me a warm drink because it was a cold winter afternoon. She then introduced me to her son, Jimmy, and tears welled up in my eyes because–you guessed it—Jimmy had Cerebral

Palsy. Later that same day, I brought my three friends to meet Jimmy and his mother. Their reactions were the same as mine.

Jimmy's mother did not have to say much. She knew we realized that we had been caught red-handed and she calmly told us that what we were doing was inappropriate, illegal, and unethical. We offered to give her the money, though I do not remember if she took it or not. I do remember she said she would see us again very soon.

The following day, the four of us were called out of class and told to report to the principal's office. We knew that we were in big trouble when we walked in and Jimmy's mother was in his office. The principal asked, "Are these the boys?"

She replied firmly, "Yes."

We thought "game over" and expected to be immediately arrested or expelled from school. Then Jimmy's mother looked at us, smiled warmly, and stated that the four of us had been polite to both Jimmy and her. She then told our principal that she expected us to continue to raise money for Cerebral Palsy and hopefully receive recognition for our efforts.

The four of us were wrong, but God used Jimmy and his mother to bring us into His corrective plan. We were way over the line. We were frauds who were stealing from our neighbors. At that moment I realized God had intervened on our behalf and prevented us from moving forward on a path that could have led us in a totally wrong direction. I went home and said the Our Father, Hail Mary, Glory Be, and Act of Contrition that I had been taught by Fr. Masterson and the nuns, followed by the commitment to not do wrong like this again.

It also made me much more conscious about what my "friends" wanted me to participate in, so I began to think about how many people really needed help in this world. God was showing me the extent He would go to in order to bring those who will listen back into His plan. He used other people to influence our lives in big ways. So, thanks to Jimmy's mother for her kindness and insights. Rather than ruining us, she had the wisdom to reclaim us, just as Jesus reclaimed the thief on Calvary.

Scripture Passage:

Internalize Corinthians 13:1.
> *Why is love so important as you travel down life's journey?*
> *How would you describe the kind of love this verse is talking about?*
> *Do you exemplify God's love to others?*
> *Is God's love selfish or serving others?*

Golden Nugget:

God has long-term plans for you that can very easily get derailed by youthful stupidity and running the streets with the wrong crowd. God will send those to help guide and influence you if you will let them and pay attention to their offered wisdom.

-4-

THE THIRD RAIL

grew up just one block from the Long Island Railroad. We played in
the empty lots immediately next to the railroad tracks at the Bayside
Rail Road Station and under the passenger platforms while the trains were
passing. Crazy? Yes! Dangerous? Yes! The theory was unless you heard the
"click," there was no electricity running through the third rail. We were
fools and believed that theory, so the challenge was to actually put your
hand on it with your palm up as a safety measure. As I write this, I get
a cold chill and a sick feeling because this was actually Russian roulette.
We could have died before the age of thirteen from this foolish behavior.

One day while I was walking to school, I began to cross the railroad
tracks. Seeing an iron bar on the ground, without thinking I picked it up
and tossed it onto the third rail. I had only taken about twenty steps when
the bar exploded, causing me to break out into a sweat and start shaking
all over. That ended my third rail contacts!

God gave me a wakeup call that day. I knew what I had been doing
was both stupid and dangerous, I had also lied to my parents, who, on

numerous occasions, had warned me about the dangers of playing near the railroad tracks. If they knew I was playing Russian roulette with the third rail, I cannot even imagine how angry they would have been. The explosion of the metal bar put the fear of God in me as I realized I was lucky to be alive. God had an interesting way of blasting through my ignorance. Even at that young age, I began to appreciate the gift of life realizing how close I had come to losing mine.

I was beginning to see for myself that God does what God does to teach us what we really need to learn and that I had a lot more yet to learn.

Scripture Passages:

Ingest Romans 1:1-18 and 2:16.
> *Is God aware of what you are doing even when others are not?*
> *How do you know?*
> *Have you ever thought you could hide your actions from God?*
> *What do you think about that idea now?*
> *How are you going to do things differently from now on?*

Golden Nugget:

I started to see a God-led pattern in my life as I reviewed my life. My introduction to Catholicism, my folly of fraudulently collecting for Cerebral Palsy, and my near death encounter with the third rail are just a few "markers" on my youthful journey that awakened an awareness in me of how God intervenes in one's life when we least expect it. We must be awake, aware, and always ready to think and learn about what and why God does these things.

CONTINUING EDUCATION

-5-

HOLY CROSS HIGH SCHOOL

In September of 1954, I was a thirteen-year-old eighth grader. During that year, work was underway to open Holy Cross High School in Flushing, Queens, New York City. My mother had gone to numerous meetings at the Flushing Armory, and met the Brothers of Holy Cross, the CSCs who had founded many marvelous high schools, colleges and universities, the most famous of which is The University of Notre Dame.

My mother wanted me to attend Holy Cross High School (HCHS), but I wanted to go to Bayside High School with my running buddies from PS 130. As time passed, and to please my mother, I agreed to take the entrance exam. On the morning of the exam, my parents had a significant disagreement as to where I should attend high school. My mother called my uncle, Al Toscani; we drove to his home and then he took me to the test site. I was nervous, frustrated, angry, and scared.

Those feelings got more intense as I spoke with people and other boys taking the entrance exam. I quickly realized that I was "the other" because very few public grammar school students were taking the test. When the test was distributed and I read the questions, "the bottom fell out" as I realized I was in deep water and about to drown. My eight years of non-learning, which was my own fault, had caught up with me because I knew few if any answers. Rather than continue the pain, I just wrote down various responses, turned in the test, and left.

The result was no surprise. I failed! In my mind, however, it was okay because now I could go to Bayside High School and my parents could stop arguing, at least over that issue. Then, in the winter of 1954-55, a letter arrived from HCHS stating that I had been accepted as a conditional student. The conditional part was expected, but student made me very edgy.

As the late Paul Harvey would say, "Here's the rest of the story." My mother had gone to the CSC brothers and pleaded for me to be accepted because she "knew" three things. First, I had not done well in elementary school. Second, I had potential as a student and leader. Third, deep down, I was a good kid who needed a chance in life. What my mother did for me back then was the key that opened the door to countless other opportunities throughout my entire life.

The rest, as they say, was history, but not in the way it sounds. Why? Well, in my first marking period I had F's or D's in Latin, algebra, biology, and English with passing grades in history and religion. I was still an academic train wreck and felt as though I had "traveled the third rail."

The brothers said I could either stay in my current classes, but if I got any more F's or D's I would be dismissed from HCHS or I could "drop back" to the general curriculum and learn what was necessary. Then if my performance was good enough, I could be admitted into the late college prep curriculum in my junior year. I took the general curriculum alternative, especially since at that time college was way out of my realm of reality. Neither of my parents had a high school diploma. I had not read a book from cover to cover in eight years of elementary school, and I had more

F's than most people at HCHS got in their entire career. However, I did actually start to think about a late college prep possibility; it was somewhat absurd but true.

My next three-and-a-half years at HCHS were marvelous. As time went on, I learned how to study and earned progressively better grades, developed lifelong friendships with terrific and loyal classmates, played basketball, participated in track field events, was the two time captain of our football team, made all-city, earned a series of scholarship offers, was a proud member if the inaugural graduating class in 1959, and was fortunate to be accepted to the College of the Holy Cross in Worcester, MA. I stayed out of trouble 95 percent of the time and became a class leader, developed a stronger faith dimension to my daily life, and continued to offer thanks to key people who were role models and really changed my life.

They were Brother John Donoghue, CSC, our principal; Mr. Walter Rooney, the first basketball coach at HCHS; Mr. Bill Stetter and Mr. Gerry Begley, the first football coaches at HCHS; numerous CSC brothers who lived at the high school and devoted their lives to all of us; significant lay teachers who worked tirelessly to be sure that the first class (and following classes) from HCHS were successful; Brother Maurus O'Malley, CSC, who authorized my conditional acceptance to HCHS; and numerous classmates who are still very close friends for plus fifty-five years.

God was teaching me lessons through academics, discipline, sports, faith, interpersonal relationships, sacrifice, helping others, creative thinking, leadership, the value of hard work, and time management. I loved HCHS, and I still respect and admire the CSCs, knowing that without them nothing else would have happened the way it has in my life since.

I owe the CSCs a lifetime of gratitude because they helped me learn that with the right environment and a willingness to respond to one's potential, a person develops style, substance, and his or her life can change for the better.

Scripture Passage:

Ponder Acts 4:13.
What stood out about Peter and John?
What did other people feel made the difference in them?
Do people say that about you?

Golden Nugget:

*The Word of God works in mysterious ways. Like most people, I did not come close to "seeing" what was going on at the time or the consequences possible in the future. There was always a sense of urgency to reach for something more than what I was doing with my life. I did not realize what it was until I recently saw a program about Coach Lou Holtz who explained his acronym for the word "win," **What's Important Now**.*

> *W.I.N. in the classroom.*
> *W.I.N. in prayer.*
> *W.I.N. in interpersonal relationships.*
> *W.I.N. in helping others.*

-6-

GUARDIAN ANGEL

It was a cold winter night in the late 1950s or early 1960s. The phone rang. The call was from one of my friends from Bayside West, near 32nd Avenue, where most of the dangerous Zombies gang lived. Most of the Zombies were a few years older than me, but my friend and three others from Bayside West were sometimes identified as "junior" Zombies.

I had played youth basketball, baseball, and pickup football games with some of them, so I was accepted in the neighborhood, but I never sought to join the gang in any official manner.

Well, on that cold winter night my friends invited me to go out with them for a car ride and some fun. I can still remember the expression of deep concern on my mother's face. She, once again, warned me to be very careful, because she predicted, someday, these particular friends of mine would get into serious trouble.

When they arrived at our apartment, I assured my mother that I would be all right, zipped up my jacket, went down the short flight of stairs to the sidewalk, greeted my friends, and then proceeded to get into the back seat of the car. But as I pulled the door toward me I just completely could not move. They said, "Denny, close the damn door and let's get going." I still could not move and a split second later I stepped back away from the car. They were enraged and yelled at me to get in the car. I said, "No, I am not going!" They then cursed and sped down 208ᵗʰ Street toward Northern Blvd.

I went back up the steps, opened the door, and startled my mother with my reentry. She asked, "Are you okay?" I simply nodded and went to my tiny bedroom, which was actually the dining room with no door. My mother once again showed her wisdom by not asking me any more questions. Deep down, I know that I did not leave that car. I was "pulled" out of that car by a force greater than mine. My departure from the vehicle was not the result of logical teenage thinking (which is often an oxymoron), but rather the result of a powerful intervention beyond my ability to understand at the time. Some time later, my mother asked me if I had heard the morning news and I replied, "Not yet."

She then told me that my friends had been drinking\ and had broken into a grocery store. When a police officer arrived, one of them shot and killed him. I froze in my tracks. Then it hit me. The only reason I did not get into that car was because of the power of my guardian angel whom I immediately expressed thanks to via prayer. The end result was my friends were booked, tried, and convicted. They went to jail and we have had no further contact.

God has a plan for each of our lives and will protect us even when we do not deserve it. However, God expects that there will be an ROHI (Return on His Investment) in the future. I have never forgotten that night, how close to disaster my life came as a teenager, and also how much I owe God and my guardian angel. Sharing this story is part of repaying my debt regarding God's ROHI.

From that point on, I tried to follow the rules and listen to my elders be they my parents, teachers, coaches, nuns, brothers, priests, or people who were just older and wiser than me. I also tried to influence others both girls and boys to steer clear of gangs and street violence. Years later, in the summer of 1963, after I graduated from college and before I went into the Marine Corps, I volunteered to work at Nativity Mission Center in Lower Manhattan with kids who lacked good opportunities and who were prone to gang memberships. That was also an ROHI and that summer proved to be one of the most meaningful experiences of my life.

Scripture Passages:

Consider Revelation 1:1-2, 10:1-2, 12:1-17.
What have you learned about angels from these verses?
Have you ever had an experience where you were saved from making
a poor decision though you did not understand it at the time?

Golden Nugget:

This close call taught me to listen to my inner voice, my conscience. I believe I have a guardian angel and sufficient faith to trust the spiritual intervention process.

God has plans for you and He will sometimes protect you beyond your understanding to make sure His plan prevails.

-7-

HOLY CROSS COLLEGE

I was sure that I wanted to go to college and hoped that I was academically ready.

The first time that I took my SAT test, the answer was "not ready" because I never did well on those types of standardized exams. So, I dropped out of basketball and other extra-curricular activities and took the SAT prep course. Then I also studied math, science, English, and history on my own for countless hours. The next time I took the SAT test, I had more than qualifying scores and accepted recruiting trips from Yale, Xavier (Ohio), the University of Virginia, and the College of the Holy Cross.

I started my career at Holy Cross as a student athlete in August of 1959. Once classes began, after preseason football practice, I quickly learned two things: how hard the curriculum really was at The Cross, and how much I had to improve as a football player if I ever expected to be a varsity starter during the next three years.

The academic lesson was loud and clear because during the first marking period I was, once again, on the brink with five C's in math, economics, English, history and Naval Science, and a D in theology. This meant that I was just below a 2.00 GPA and that was far from acceptable at Holy Cross. I then sought and received permission from a group of serious upper class pre-med students to join their study group. My grades immediately improved because they studied with intensity, and I learned to do the same thing.

The second lesson was equally loud and clear when we scrimmaged against the varsity. Every time that happened, I lined up across from one of the HC all-time greats, Vince Promuto, and the results were always the same—I got beat up. Vince went on to have a great NFL career with the Washington Redskins. Playing against him made me much tougher and more determined to do my best which proved to be good enough.

The athletic philosophy of Holy Cross has always been to have inter-collegiate competitors that are real student-athletes who are well prepared for life once their NCAA or professional sports careers have ended.

Academic and athletic success notwithstanding, the greatest lessons that I leaned in college were about communication, community, commitment, and the constant reminders that "to whom much is given much is required." This led to a deeper, life-long understanding of what the Jesuits mean by becoming "men and women for others," especially for the sick, poor and under-served.

Through lessons learned at Holy Cross and beyond, I came to the realization that if you say the words "I believe," you better be ready to really proclaim the reality of the birth, life, teachings, suffering, death, resurrection, and ascension of Jesus Christ, otherwise there would be no Christianity, no Catholic Church, no Society of Jesus (Jesuits), no College of the Holy Cross, and no words on this page.

God was teaching me that I had to awaken to my challenges, opportunities, and responsibilities. I had one collegiate chance to do so and the "fear of failure" was a good motivation for me to strive to do my very best.

During my administrative career, I always tried to encourage everyone, especially the students, to keep a balance in their lives using the image of the cross of Christ. The top of the cross is their intellectual development. The base of the cross is their faith foundation. The two arms of the cross is their family/friends, and then all other positive constructive activities. That image helped countless students to find their balance and then grow swiftly and strongly into the person God has called them to be in life.

Scripture Passages:

Carefully consider Acts 1:1-3, 8, and 22.

Do you understand what Jesus did for you on the cross?

Do you believe it was for you?

Are you willing to take a stand and declare your belief in the one true God?

Golden Nugget:

God is a reality! There are multiple people and cultures who have different ways of knowing, loving, and worshipping God in order to gain their eternal salvation. To support them is positive and necessary. It is equally important to fight against those who force their religious beliefs on others especially via terror. This becomes a "war of ideas" and a "struggle" against "submission" that can strangle and kill Christianity and other faiths. What is needed is not more armed conflict. What is needed is a worldwide, continuous summit of religious leaders who can discuss, discern, reconcile, and lead for peace, not terror and war.

PASSAGE 3

CAREER CHOICES

-8-

USMC

Let me start by saying that I am proud to be a United States Marine. Yes, I use present tense because, "Once a Marine, Always a Marine." I served as an officer on active duty from 1963-1966, and then completed my inactive reserve time, and some years later, I was in a VTU (Volunteer Training Unit).

However, prior to 1963, I was a midshipman in the Naval ROTC at Holy Cross. At the end of my junior year, I did a summer cruise aboard the USS Bronson DD 868, shipping out of Newport, RI. Although my naval training went very well, I decided to apply for an inter-service transfer to the USMC. Eventually, this was authorized, and it meant that upon my college graduation I would have to do six more weeks of pre-commission training at Quantico, VA. It also meant a third year of active duty, all of which I willingly agreed to do.

As history shows, in the early 1960s, we had military advisors in Vietnam, but at that time it was not something that seemed to be of imminent consequence. There are many USMC related stories, but I will share only two. One had to do with personal thought and preference, and the other was more related to government and military policies; as you will see, they were interrelated.

All second lieutenants at The Basic School were, and I assume still are, given the opportunity to state their MOS (Military Occupational Specialty) preferences. I chose intelligence, disbursing, and supply. Shortly thereafter, I found myself "front and center" with the Commanding Officer of The Basic School, Col. Jonas M. Platt, who made an official inquiry pertaining to my MOS preferences. Col. Platt told me that I was a "Marine's Marine" and that I was a natural troop commander. This was certainly high praise coming from the CO of The Basic School, but in view of that fact he questioned me as to why I had not chosen infantry, artillery, tanks, motor transport, communications, etc., I responded that I had grown up in NYC, played sports for years (including on the 1963 Quantico Marines Armed Forces National Championship football team), and in college the Jesuits had always inspired me to get as much education as possible; thus, I wanted to do something slightly different as I served my country.

Col. Platt was an outstanding officer, and in the USMC parlance, it does not get any better than outstanding. He was also a true gentleman and did not order me to change my MOS preferences. He did tell me, however, that I might very well be assigned to 03 infantry status and not 30 supply status. I said that I would do whatever was necessary for the greater good of the US Marine Corps. When I was dismissed from the meeting, we parted on the basis of mutual understanding and respect. Shortly thereafter, I received a supply status and was scheduled for Supply School at Camp Lejeune, NC, in the winter of 1964.

Prior to that time, however, I played football for the second and last time for the Quantico Marines. Our last game was against the San Diego

Marines in Balboa Stadium. Following the game, I needed medical attention for a foot injury and consequently arrived late for the team banquet and awards ceremony. We were all in civilian clothes, so when I sat down I had no idea who I was sitting next to. The man next to me and I were having a marvelous conversation. Moreover, I couldn't figure out why my teammates sitting across the table from me were trying to wave me off.

Shortly thereafter, there was an announcement inviting the Commanding General of the US Marine Corps Recruit Depot to please come forward for the presentations. Well, when the man sitting next to me stood up and moved forward, I almost "fell out!" I had been in conversation with and back slapping (probably because of the pain killers I had been given at the hospital, plus the two beers that I had been drinking) Major General Bruno A. Hochmuth. I was in shock!

When General Hochmuth came back to our table, I was both apologetic and "squared away!" But just like Col. Platt, General Hochmuth was a perfect gentlemen and an outstanding Marine officer. So, he told me to relax and asked me where my orders were taking me. I told him that I was scheduled for Supply School in Camp Lejeune, NC. Then the shock continued because he stated that once I graduated he would like me to be under his command at MCRD San Diego, and that is exactly what happened approximately four months later.

Shortly after our arrival in San Diego, Monica gave birth to our first son, Patrick, at the Balboa Naval Hospital on May 23, 1965. By this time, I had also decided to start law school at the University of San Diego, which I did in August of 1965. It was also clear that because of the Gulf of Tonkin Resolution, we were about to experience a significantly increased military commitment in Vietnam.

Unexpectedly, in June of 1965, two other Lieutenants and I were summoned to General Hochmuth's office. He informed us that the First

Marine Division at Camp Pendleton, CA, was being immediately mobilized. He also told us that he had a special set of orders directing him to significantly increase the number of MCRD recruits during the next year. Then there was a third shock as General Hochmuth informed us that our names had been removed from the mobilization manifest and were assigned to the MCRD Headquarters & Service Battalion in order to assist with the supply and troop training of the recruits. Thus, we may have been the only three junior officers during that specific time that did not serve "in country." We found that hard to understand and accept, but we had nothing to do with the decision, except we were all supply officers. As mentioned previously, this is the part of the USMC story that is personal. Now for the second part that is more oriented toward policy.

While working in the H&S Battalion and the troop training regiment at MCRD, I was summoned to a meeting with a USMC major, who was what is honorably and admirably referred to as a Mustang, meaning he had originally served with distinction as an enlisted Marine and had earned his way all the way up to field grade officer. His record showed that he had served during the end of WWII, then in Korea, and was one of the original advisors in Vietnam.

He had studied my Service Record Book, and realized that I had been a history major and done student teaching while at Holy Cross. He assigned me to be the Assistant Base Education Officer reporting directly to him. My assignment was to write a tactical lesson plan that could be replicated for each new series of enlisted recruits at MCRD San Diego regarding the tactics needed in order to defeat the enemy in Vietnam.

From the base PIO (Public Information Office), I requested and received volumes of information pertaining to prior military incursions into Vietnam with special emphasis regarding the efforts by the Chinese, Japanese, and French. The startling revelation was that none of them had been successful. Consequently, I started to get deeply concerned as to why we were there and how to fight and win the military battle. I also realized that in view of the order that the major had given me, I was facing both a moral and ethical dilemma. My decision was to write the lesson plan to the best of my ability, but with cautious reservations.

Within a few days, I reported back to the major and presented the tactical lesson plan which he carefully reviewed and then complimented me for its accuracy and value. Then correctly sensing that something was not right, he asked me what was wrong.

I took a deep breath and asked him, "May I speak freely, Sir?"

He gave me an affirmative response. When this happens in the US Marine Corps, you can say anything that you choose without fear of retribution, so I was cleared to go ahead and voice my concerns. I told the major that my research had convinced me that:

1. I did not believe we could ever win a war of attrition.
2. I did not support the philosophy of fortified hamlets.
3. I did not agree with a search and destroy philosophy.
4. I did not favor the way we were expected to employ The Rules of Engagement.
5. I would have serious reservations complying with The Rules of Engagement if I was a platoon commander in country.

By this time, I could readily see that the major was extremely angry and he said with severe earnestness, "Anything else?"

I responded respectfully, "No, Sir."

Then he clearly informed me that we were back on the official record and asked me if I understood.

I responded, "Yes, Sir."

Then he asked me if I had not requested and received his permission to "speak freely" what would he have done to me?

I said, "Sir, you would probably have charged me with sedition."

He said, "You do understand, don't you?"

I responded once again, "Yes, Sir."

Well, he told me that I was going to give that tactical lesson plan the way, I designed it for as long as necessary to which I gave a final, "Yes, Sir."

I was then summarily dismissed.

Two days later I gave that presentation to about three hundred Marine recruits as written.

After I finished, from behind the auditorium curtain I heard, "Lieutenant Golden."

I turned to face the major.

He said, "You gave it straight."

I said, "Yes, Sir."

He asked, "Any questions?"

I said, "No, Sir."

But I did follow up with, "Sir, you will not give me permission to speak freely, so I will not make that request." He nodded then I said, "Sir, with all due respect, I took an oath of office to defend the Constitution from all enemies both foreign and domestic, but I did not take an oath of office to fight in a war with priority restrictions that I believe may help the enemy more than our own troops."

The major looked at me one more time, and with steel cold eyes, said, "Dismissed."

I said, "Sir, Yes, Sir," saluted and departed.

The next day, I was pulled off the tactical education assignment and expected to be sent to Vietnam a few days later. That never happened, and I concluded my tour of active duty on August 31, 1966.

After years of personal, emotional dissonance about not serving in Vietnam, plus years of knowing and loving those who died or lived with severe wounds because of what was detrimental to us, I have finally come to peace with this moral dilemma. God has given me the courage to share this story with the hopeful expectation that things like this will cease so that when our military is engaged in a conflict, it will at least be a fair fight.

I pray that my story will help others faced with similar ethical and moral dilemmas to not just blindly trust the people in power. May the people in power come to realize they are responsible for their policies. Too many people "go along" and do not challenge and stand up for what they believe. History clearly shows that many military leaders and the highest elected officials in the country were dead wrong about many aspects about the Vietnam conflict. Many of our men and women in the military paid the ultimate price for those bad decisions.

Scripture Passage:

Carefully consider the warning issued by God in Micah 2:1-4.
What is God warning against in these verses?
Read what God says about those who lead His people astray in Micah 3:1-5.
What punishment do they face?
Ecclesiastes 3:1-8 says there is a time   .
What does this say about war?

Golden Nugget:

My experiences in the military taught me it is our responsibility to seek, ask, clarify, define, understand, and collaborate the decisions made by our *leaders on the basis of **truth—God's truth.** I am still and always will be proud to be a Marine. I love the Marine Corps. When allowed to defend our country properly, we know how to do it and we will prevail.*

-9-

BOSTON PATRIOTS

My tour of duty in the Marine Corps concluded in August, 1966. By that time, the armed conflict in Vietnam was becoming both public and problematic in many different ways. I thought of staying on active duty, but I also wanted to fulfill my dream of playing professional football, having been drafted by the Dallas Cowboys in 1963.

I started law school at the University of San Diego because I had a desire to become a lawyer and to practice law back in New England. When the then Boston Patriots came to San Diego to play the Chargers during the 1965 season, I met with their Head Coach, Mike Holovak, and he offered me a free agent tryout and contract for the summer of 1966, which I gladly accepted.

The last preseason exhibition game was held in Mobile, Alabama, in late August of 1966, and that trip changed my focus from the field of play to the field of no further delay. During training camp, I became close friends with the late, great fullback, Jim Nance, from Syracuse University. Jim told me that he was uncomfortable playing in the deep South, because when Syracuse was in a bowl game, he and the other black players on the team had an extremely hard time dealing with the segregation laws. This resulted in them being shunned and disrespected by many people, including their opposing players.

With this in mind, and the desire to relax the night before the game, Jim and I decided to leave the hotel and walk a few blocks to a movie theater. I went to the ticket booth to buy the tickets. The man was initially very polite until I tried to purchase two tickets. Then his demeanor changed and he asked me who the second ticket was for. Having grown up in New York City, I thought that this was a rude question, but then I immediately realized that this was a segregation question; I was right.

The white ticket seller told me that if the other ticket was for the man standing a few paces behind me, that he would sell me the tickets, but that the black man would have to sit in the colored section of the theater. I was enraged. Because I was still on USMC active duty, I told the ticket seller that I considered him to be a domestic enemy of the US Constitution, and I strongly suggested that he sell me both tickets and that we would sit together in that theater. He then realized I was serious, he was shocked as I glared him.

Just then I felt a hand on my shoulder, and I spun around ready to throw a punch if necessary, but it was the hand of Jim Nance, who then said to me, "Denny, it's not worth the trouble. Let's get out of here."

To which I responded, "If that is what you want it's fine with me."

That happened almost fifty years ago, but I have never forgotten how we both felt that night in Mobile, Alabama.

However, it didn't end there. The next day was game day. We had a light workout, after which Coach Holovak made it explicitly clear that he wanted all of us to be in the dining room at a specific time. I was and still am one of those people who not only tries to time, but who likes to be early for any and all commitments. So, with sufficient lead time, my roommate, Doug Satcher, and I were leaving our hotel room for the team meal when the phone rang.

Doug answered the phone, it was my wife, Monica. Doug handed me the phone, and I began my conversation with Monica. In essence, she called to wish me good luck in the game and to tell me that our fifteen-month-old son, Patrick, was sick with a very high fever. Since Monica was an RN, I knew that she would do all the right things for Pat. Then I assured her I would be home as soon as possible following our post-game flight back to Boston.

The entire conversation probably took five minutes, but by the time I left the room, took the elevator to the lobby level, and entered the dining room, over ten minutes had elapsed. Although pregame meals are never very noisy, there was an unusual collective quiet in the dining room that caught me off guard. Preoccupied because I knew that I was late and had to check in with the coaching staff, I entered the dining room. My position coach, Jess Richardson, waved me over to the table and immediately asked why I was late. When I explained the circumstances, he said, "Okay," but that I also had to explain it to Coach Holovak. Thankfully, he too was very understanding.

Just then, a woman who worked for the hotel dining services politely asked me if I was with the team. When I answered *yes*, she said for me to wait there and that she would set a place for me. Then, once again, I became acutely aware of the "screaming silence" in the dining room. Then it hit me. As I looked around the dining area, I saw that the white players were on one side of the room and that the "colored" players were on the other side. In a couple of hours we could run, block, tackle, pass, catch, kick, and win or lose together, but we could not eat together.

My tenseness was now gone and my action switch was activated. As I looked to my immediate right, there was an empty seat so I asked if it was all right for me to sit down. My teammates didn't look up, and there was no response, so I asked again and this time louder.

This time the leader, Houston Antwine said, "We don't mind if you don't mind."

So, I pulled out my chair and began to sit down with great players and even greater people like Larry Garron, J.D. Garrett, Jim Nance, Jim Lee Hunt, Donnie Webb, and others.

Just then the hostess of the dining room rushed over and said, "Sir, your seat is on the other side of the dining room."

To which I responded, "No Ma'am, my seat is right here with my friends so please bring me my meal."

The original quietude and "screaming silence" were now changed into collective shock. What I now refer to as the Mobile Malaise played a great part in transforming my later higher education career into a commitment to justice, diversity, and civil rights. This type of racial discrimination was not new to these gentleman, but I could not stand the racism, intolerance, discrimination, and bigotry, so I went on to try to do something about it.

Though I honestly thought that I had made the team, I was the last one cut two days before the aforementioned game in Mobile, Alabama. There were only two defensive ends on the team and they were both excellent. One was the late, Bob Dee, and the other was, Larry Eisenhaer. So, I asked Coach Holovak to let me make the trip as the third defensive end and he agreed to do so. Had Coach Holovak not given his permission, neither of those two experiences that ignited a fire of commitment within my soul would have happened.

After returning to Boston, I drove to NYC and had a great tryout with New York Giant NFL Hall of Fame Defensive End, Andy Robestelli.

Coach Robestelli assured me that based upon both film analysis and on field play, I was ready for professional football and he offered me a contract. The next day, after thought and prayer, I turned down the contract and began my forty-eight-year career in higher education.

To this Coach Robestelli said, "Good for you. Most pros only last three to five years. You are making a career decision—so do it and don't look back."

My official football playing days were over at twenty-four, but I did go on to coach football at both the College of the Holy Cross (for three years) and at Framingham State College (for ten years). During this time, I was a fulltime administrator as well as a graduate student. During those years, our second son, Dennis, and our daughter, Kristine, were born in 1967 and 1973 respectively. Monica, as always, was extremely supportive, loving, and held it all together.

To sum up, I am convinced that God works in mysterious ways. As Saint John Paul II said in matters of consequence and importance, "There is no such thing as mere coincidence." In my life, that certainly includes football both inside and outside the field of play.

Scripture Passage:

Consider David's prayer in Psalm 25:1-5.
Where should you put your trust?
Who gives you hope and guidance through life?
Whose truths should you base your decisions on?

Golden Nugget:

When we determine to live by God's truths and walk His paths, we see everyone through His eyes. To Him we are all His children. Romans 10:11-12 says there is no difference between us, He is Lord of all and richly blesses all who call on Him.

-10-

BOSTON COLLEGE DOCTORATE

I n the early 1970s, Monica and I were living in Hopkinton, Massachusetts, with our three young children. I was the dean of students and head football coach at Framingham State College. I was also, and doctoral candidate in Higher Education Administration at Boston College.

Not being one to waste time, I had already completed three chapters of my dissertation pertaining to the Delphi research techniques. One morning, I awoke and clearly realized that this was not what I really wanted to study. This all gave me significant concern because the pragmatic means to the end was to get my research topic approved, do the study, write the chapters, pass the dissertation defense, and transition from Mr. or Dr.

Consequently, I met with my dissertation advisor, Dr. Mary Kinnane, to change my topic. Explaining I could not continue because I really wanted to do research on higher education administration, I obtained her approval and that of Dean Mary Griffin. Then I respectfully approached and secured the approval of Dr. Evan R. "Van" Collins to be my new dissertation advisor. Dr. Collins, a university president for over twenty years, and who had been my instructor for three courses, so I had extreme confidence in this outstanding educator.

This new dissertation was focused on the eleven state colleges in Massachusetts, which I believe are now all universities. The research was titled, "An Analysis of the Perceptions Held by Elected Student Government Officers, Elected Faculty Officers and Administrators." I was passionate about this topic and worked triple time to get it done, the actual delay in finishing was only six months, and my dissertation was approved in 1974. Both the methodology and the findings from that study proved to be of ongoing value throughout my career in higher education. Those were hard years in terms of time and sacrifice, but in the long run, they were well worth the effort.

Scripture Passage:

Invest time studying the wisdom of Proverbs.
Proverbs 1:2-4 says they were written for:

_____   _____

_____   _____

_____   _____

_____   _____

Golden Nugget:

As I matured in my walk of life, I realized one can do almost anything one puts his or her mind and heart to, but that time is a very precious natural resource that must be invested wisely. In both personal and professional decision making, what a person is passionate about is usually what God is leading one to invest time and energy in.

-11-

THE CALLING TO UNIVERSITY PRESIDENCY

Although both my parents were smart enough, neither of them graduated from high school. My educational journey was very different. In 1959, I was a member of the first class to graduate from Holy Cross High School. As a student-athlete, college had become a possibility, which I completed at the College of the Holy Cross in 1963. Although drafted by the Dallas Cowboys of the NFL, I chose to serve my country as an officer in the U.S. Marine Corps. While on active duty, I realized that I wanted to continue my love of learning, took both an extension course from the University of Virginia, and attended, but did not complete, law school at the University of San Diego, CA.

After tryouts with the Boston Patriots and the NY Giants, I passed up a football contract to take a position as assistant to the Dean of Men at Holy Cross. New York Giants all-time great and member of the NFL Hall of Fame, Andy Robestelli, told me that I was ready to play in the NFL.

However, as a twenty-four-year-old rookie just coming off active duty in the Marine Corps, my view of life had changed.

So, after receiving my masters in guidance and psychology from Assumption College in 1969.I completed my doctorate in higher education administration at Boston College in 1974. The point of all of this is that although I was far from an honor student and what others would call an intellectual, I was a very hard-working, determined student. God was calling me to become a leader in higher education. I heard God's call, followed through, and tried faithfully to serve Him in higher education for forty-eight years.

My calling brought me to five different institutions, with my presidency at Fontbonne University being the highest and most significant "calling" of them all. During those years, I somehow realized that I was being led, helped, guided, and supported by God every day. Certainly there were times when I ran out of patience and made the wrong decisions, but I always apologized, took responsibility for what I had or had not done, then tried to move forward in a positive manner. As I often say to those who aspire for the presidency, you may never know the fruits of your labor during your lifetime, so just focus on doing the next right thing all the time and trust God all the way.

Scripture Passage:

Glean guidance from Habakkuk 2:1-3.

When you hear God's call, are you hardening your heart against what He is telling you to do?

What is God calling you to do?

Golden Nugget:

If you really believe in God's presence, if you are really a follower of Jesus Christ, if you really want to make positive and significant differences in people's lives, then listen to God's calling and respond with, "Yes!"

If you find inner peace and tranquility even in an environment or vocation that is demanding and complex, you are in the right place at the right time and you will be able to do so because you are following God's calling.

MENTORS AND MANTRAS THAT MOTIVATE

-12-

MENTORS THAT MATTER

When you are a young professional with a family and your career is higher education administration, you are well advised to have good mentors. You may ask certain people to be your mentors and at other times seasoned professionals may offer. Sometimes there is no social contract, but because of your observations of what certain people are doing, they become your unofficial mentors. Regardless of how it happens, the key is to study how they work, relate to people—particularly under pressure, and then decide whether or not their decisions foster the greatest common good.

In my case, as an undergraduate student at the College of the Holy Cross, three Jesuit priests reached out to mentor me when I needed it the most. The first was my freshman math teacher Fr. Raymond J. Swords, S.J., who provided me excellent academic mentoring. Fr. Swords then became an outstanding president at The Cross. Spiritual mentoring came from Fr. Joseph J. La Bran, S.J., who introduced me to The Spiritual Exercises of St. Ignatius Loyola, as well as many other spiritual and sacrificial realities.

I also had the good fortune to learn from and later work for Fr. Charles J. Dunn, S.J., who was our Dean of Men (Holy Cross was still an all-male college in the early 1960s). Fr. Dunn set very high standards for our behavior as well as for our care and concern for others. To be influenced and mentored by people of this caliber was a true gift from God for this first generation college student.

Upon my honorable discharge from the U.S. Marine Corps in 1966, I started my higher education career back at Holy Cross as the assistant to Fr. James Barry, S. J., Dean of Men. By that time, Fr. Dunn was the first Vice President of Student Affairs at Holy Cross.

In July of 1969, I was offered and accepted the position as the first ever Dean of Students at Framingham State College, now Framingham State University. During my time at Framingham State that position became VP for Student Affairs. My direct report was always to President Dr. D. Justin McCarthy. Once again, I was extremely fortunate to have an excellent mentor in Dr. McCarthy, who taught me about the greatness of public higher education.

After thirteen years at Framingham, I became the VP for Student Affairs at Duquesne University in Pittsburgh, PA. My family and I loved Duquesne and our time in Western Pennsylvania. I learned many positive things, but I also learned many lessons about what senior administration should and should not do. In particular, I learned that position power must not trump personal, ethical power, especially if the former is not used for the greatest good of the university.

During the early to middle 1980s, Duquesne experienced very serious senior administrative turmoil. Chosing not to emulate the prevailing administrative ethos, I was fired and had to really think deeply about the meaning of mentorship. Subsequently, after a presidential departure and an interim presidential appointment, a new efficient and effective president was appointed and Duquesne reclaimed her rightful place of honor in the ranks of Catholic higher education.

During my personal time of unemployment, a friend and mentor, Dr. Andrea C. McAleenan, arranged for me to work *pro tem* and *pro bono* with, Dr. Reid Carpenter, at the Pittsburgh Leadership Foundation. During that time, the concept of reaching out and helping others really became personal. I learned that just when I thought I could not go on, I turned to constant prayer. Prayers do get answered! It was during my very last day at the PLF that the phone rang, and subsequent to a very comprehensive interview process and complete background check (especially in regard to Duquesne), I was offered the position of VP for Student Affairs of the University of Louisville. This was a quantum leap forward both personally and professionally. With tears of thanksgiving streaming down my face, I immediately accepted the position and thanked God abundantly.

For the next seven years, I worked with pride and passion for UofL. During that time, I was also elected president of NASPA (National Association of Student Personnel Administrators) which gave me both the opportunity and the responsibility to look at student life from local, regional, national, and international perspectives. While at UofL, I reported directly to our distinguished president, Dr. Donald C. Swain, who was my quintessential presidential mentor, and when Dr. Swain said I was ready to become a president, it was one of the most memorable days of my life. Thereafter, I set out on the pathway, as Robert Frost said, "...less traveled," that really did make all the difference.

During my subsequent nearly twenty years as president at Fontbonne College (now Fontbonne University), when difficult situations arose, and many did, I would ask myself: what would Fr. Swords, Dr. McCarthy or Dr. Swain do? Then I would get centered, calm, and clear, and move ahead. People can judge for themselves, but I honestly believe that their mentorship gave me the ability to make decisions that were in the best interests of Fontbonne, especially for the students.

God was also teaching me to look at the consequences of leadership and to choose the right type of leaders to follow. Sometimes, we have adequate time while other times the process is compressed, but the end result must be focused on the greatest possible good. God was also teaching me that a leader cannot preach to an astute university community–especially not to a highly gifted faculty. What you can do is collaborate and commit to shared governance. By so doing, your decisions become your "sermons" as do your style, substance, and results. You are responsible for those results and will be judged accordingly.

I decided that consultation and open communication plus complete transparency were the way to go. A primary example was the establishment of All Campus Meetings, which were held shortly after every meeting of the Board of Trustees. Faculty, students, staff, and administration were welcomed to these meetings and frequently the attendance was standing room only. During those meetings, the vice presidents and I would share everything possible with the university community so that all constituents were well informed. As Dr. Swain would say, "They put on their university hats," not just their unit hats for the greatest good possible. What the leader does and how the university president operates really does matter and can strengthen or damage the university.

As a university president, I also found I was always on duty both on and off campus. People frequently judge the entire campus by how the president communicates, relates, and acts in private as well as in public. The university president must always be careful not to embarrass himself or herself or to harm the reputation of the university in any way, because once that happens it takes a very long time to recover.

Scripture Passage:

Jesus gave us Matthew 7:12, which many refer to as the Golden Rule.
What does this mean to you if you are in a leadership position?
How should you treat those in positions above you and below you?
Who has God given you as mentors?

Golden Nugget:

Emulate only the very best and thank them accordingly. Choose your mentors wisely.

-13-

PUMPKINS AND THE GRAND CANYON

W hile at Framingham State College (1969-1982), I reported directly to our president, Dr. D. Justin McCarthy. During freshman orientation, I remember Dr. McCarthy thanking the parents for trusting us with their most precious possessions, their sons and daughters. He then assured them that change would occur and that by working together we could mutually help their sons and daughters to maximize their potential.

That was all well received, and then he issued them a warning not about academics or improper behavior. To their surprise, the warning was to remind them that Halloween would be coming soon. Puzzled? So was I the first time I heard it as a newly appointed twenty-seven-year-old Dean of Students. Dr. McCarthy's warning was about the time needed for mature growth and development as he reminded both students and parents that pumpkins and Halloween come together once a year and that pumpkins take only one growing season—then they are gone.

He then went on to say that at Framingham State, we were not really interested in having our students or parents commit to only one pumpkin-like growing season. To the contrary, we wanted them to grow much stronger, deeper, taller, and longer like great oak trees and to become people with strong roots and lasting presence. To do this takes much more time and care, but the lifelong results are well worth the effort. Year after year people were inspired by what we called the "pumpkin and oak tree" message at Framingham State and on other campuses.

In like manner, at Holy Cross College, VP for Student Affairs, Fr. Charles J. Dunn, S.J., reminded various people, this writer among them, about the Jesuit holistic philosophy of education, which encompasses mind, body, spirit, emotions, and commitment to become "men and women for others." The analogy here was the power of water. If you watch water flow over hard surfaces, you will probably see little if any short term change. In the long run, however, you may see a personal Grand Canyon like transformation. Like oak trees, this also takes time (not infrequently decades), but the individual results are well worth the time and effort. Once achieved one may benefit from what President Teddy Roosevelt said about the real Grand Canyon, "You cannot improve on it. Leave it as it is!" (Speech at the Grand Canyon, 1903).

During my career, I always tried to help both students and colleagues "become" oak trees while also encouraging them to manifest the beauty and grandeur of their personal Grand Canyon. After nearly a half century in higher education, I saw the results–it works.

God was telling me that as a teacher, coach, dean, vice president, president, and more importantly as a person, I had a responsibility to try and help others see and utilize ways and means to transform their lives, not just settle for short-term changes.

Those two simple, but powerful analogies from Dr. McCarthy and Fr. Dunn gave me a philosophical framework that affected my whole career and hopefully the lives of many others.

Scripture Passage:

Learn from the way Jesus ministered to people in Matthew 4:23-25.
Jesus preached but He also did what?
Jesus often used parables to help His listeners understand what He was trying to teach them. Read some of His parables in Matthew 13.
Why are parables and analogies so effective?

Golden Nugget:

Simple analogies or parables can and frequently do have transformative potential and power. The lives we live often speak louder than the words we "preach" at people.

-14-

MANTRAS THAT MOTIVATE

As I went through life, met more people, did more things, traveled more places, and experienced both consolation and desolation, I needed certain mantras to guide and motivate me throughout my pilgrim journey. Three of those mantras are as follows:

AMDG: *Ad Majorem Dei Gloriam* means, "For the Greater Glory of God." This is the primary purpose for the Spiritual Exercises of St. Ignatius Loyola, the founder of the Jesuits in 1540, and it is their universal belief. The Jesuits also inspire others to commit to what is referred to as The Magis or The More, thereby encouraging them to "go beyond" and do all that one is capable of doing for the good of others. The means to that end is to become "Men and Women for Others."

Learn More Be More: This is the educational mantra of Fontbonne University, where students are frequently encouraged not only to learn how to earn a living, but how to live a life which is ultimately more important. This also means that they should strive to become critical thinkers and ethical leaders for a world in need.

Freedom Is Not for Free: Since America is a Republic, we are governed by the rule of law. Those laws provide us with rights and responsibilities that are grounded in our Constitution. Now, perhaps more than ever since 1776, radical and violent extremists are threatening people worldwide. Thus, there is a price to be paid by everyone who wants to live in freedom. It is a high price that requires the vision, plan, capability, and will to fight back intellectually, morally, politically, economically, religiously, and if need be, militarily– to prevail. Jesus said, "Turn the other cheek," I am willing to do so as much as possible, but even Jesus threw people out of the temple. So when others proclaim that they will settle for nothing less than conversion, submission or death, I will fight for my freedom.

Scripture Passage:

> Jesus gave us many mantras to live by. Here are a few to begin with. Write each one out in your own words and then add more of your own as you search the Scriptures for yourself.
>
> John 13:34-35 says, _____
> John 3:6 says, _____
> John 5:30 says, _____
> Matthew 5:14-16 says, _____
> Matthew 5:44 says, _____

Golden Nugget:

> Colossians 3:23-24 gives us a wonderful wisdom nugget to live by:
> *And whatever you do, do it heartily, as to the Lord and*
> *not to men, knowing that from the Lord you will receive*

the reward of the inheritance; for you serve the Lord Christ. (NKJV)

-15-

CATHEDRAL BUILDER

Years ago a very special professional colleague of mine, Dr. Jim Hurst, former Vice President of Student Affairs at the University of Wyoming, shared the story of the cathedral builders. Obviously, I have never forgotten it; it has provided me with a "vision basis" throughout my career. The story goes like this:

A man walked by a construction site and saw three very hard workers doing exactly the same thing. Taking cut stones from a pile, covering the edges with mortar and placing them in the proper places as the structure took form.

The man asked the first laborer what he was doing and the reply was, "I'm laying stone in a row."

Upon inquiring of the second laborer, he replied "I'm building a wall."

But the third laborer stated with pride, "I'm constructing a cathedral."

All three were doing the exact same work, but only one of the three really understood the big picture and the ultimate purpose of his work. He was constructing a cathedral.

Through Jim Hurst, I believe that God intended for this story to teach me to "look beyond" what I am doing today in order to seek and hopefully find the true purpose for my life's labors and view everything, as much as possible, in terms of eternity. In all of my higher education experiences as a teacher, coach, administrator, consultant and mentor, **I tried to keep the ultimate vision of salvation in mind.** Sometimes I failed, but the effort was made nonetheless.

Scripture Passages:

Consider the analogy of the builder in Hebrews 3:3-4.
What does this passage say about whose house we are?
How does that change what you say and do even in your everyday life?
In Hebrews 11:9-10, what were Abraham, Isaac, and Jacob looking forward to?
What are you looking forward to as you go about your everyday activities?

Golden Nugget:

A story told by a friend and professional colleague has helped, guided, and inspired me for years. I am thankful for how he sowed into my life and know I have a duty to pass it along to others.

-16-

DARE TO DREAM

When you are in the world of higher education, you have both the privilege and the responsibility to engage in real thinking. This means thinking that is serious, ethical, effective, transformative in nature, and followed by action. To put this into an even larger context, I once heard someone say that such real thinking is the hardest work there is, and that's why so few people engage in it.

In the world of higher education, you are also involved with numerous discussions, meetings, seminars, webcasts, conferences, etc. At times, they can all seem to run together, and at other times one may stand out because of the significance of the people, time, place, circumstances, and theme.

Such an unforgettable event took place in Boston, Massachusetts, on April 4-7, 1982. It was during the annual NASPA Conference (National Association of Student Personnel Administrators). At that time, I was the VP for Student Affairs at Framingham State College, MA, and the conference chairperson. Because Boston was experiencing very serious and ongoing racial tension, the members of the conference committee, all close

72

friends of mine, knew that the choice for the conference theme would be extremely important.

Enter real and critical thinking, because my loyal, trusted, and highly competent professional colleague, Dr. Robert B. "Bob" Young, was our conference program chair. Bob not only understood what was needed, he created, offered, and we unanimously supported his proposed conference theme, *Dare to Dream.* The potential in those three powerful words was actualized via Bob's four transformative sub themes: Dare to Dream of a Better Life, Dare to Dream of Executive Leadership, Dare to Dream of Higher Learning, and Dare to Dream of a Humane World.

Additional commitment relating to the importance of the conference theme was evidenced by the fact that conference attendees were provided with a special and meaningful symbol which they proudly displayed. It was a brilliant red pin representing the blood kinship of humankind. The pin also displayed the olive branch of peace with differently colored leaves representing the major races on the face of the earth.

This symbol originated with the Council of Churches in the City of Boston. With both dignity and reverence they identified the symbol as the Covenant of Equity, Justice, and Harmony. I respectfully sought and received permission from the Council to use the symbol for the NASPA conference. They also gave me unconditional permission to use the Covenant pins in the future, which I did throughout the remainder of my career.

As we all know, Reverend Dr. Martin Luther King, Jr. delivered his "I Have a Dream" speech to over 250,000 civil rights supporters, in Washington, DC, on August 28, 1963. From that day forward, multiple millions have had dreams about how to make the world better and safer for all of God's people. We did our best in April of 1982, and the torch for justice and freedom continues to burn brightly in the professional and private lives of NASPA members and the students that they represent and serve on thousands of campuses across the country and beyond.

Scripture Passage:

Jesus taught the Beatitudes in Matthew 5:3-11. Each one starts with the words "Blessed are..." which, according to the Amplified Bible, means "happy, to be envied, spiritually prosperous with life, joy, and satisfaction in God's favor and salvation, regardless of their outward conditions."

Read each Beatitude and write them out in your own words, including the promise that goes with each one.

1.
2.
3.
4.
5.
6.
7.
8.

Golden Nugget:

The Dare to Dream Conference impacted my life and helped me focus on what God was calling me to do. Think of an event in your life that impacted you in a major way. Describe it and then write why it was so impactful to you.

PASSAGE 5

WHY WE DO WHAT WE DO

-17-

SERVANT LEADERSHIP

As every college and university president knows, sooner or later you are asked to explain your leadership style. The answer is frequently dependent upon how you view yourself in relation to your institution.

For example, if you come to a university that is in big financial trouble, you are expected to know what needs to be done and how to do it quickly. In such a situation, your style could be classified as a hardnosed change agent, and that may be exactly what that school needs at that time–the right fit. If one becomes the president of a more stable university, that quick fix, hardnosed change agent approach could seriously backfire– bad fit. So, the president should be extremely careful when choosing and implementing his/her leadership style. By the same token, the president must be clear and honest when it is implemented.

During my nearly twenty years as the president of Fontbonne University, my leadership style was that of a Servant-Leader. I always tried to understand and coordinate the elements of who, what, when, where, how, and why in a collaborative way via my belief in shared governance. It was also done with an understanding of the inextricable interdependence of the varied campus constituencies that simultaneously make universities both fragile and formidable. Moreover, I viewed the presidency as a sacred trust, and I always tried to put the greatest good of the students as the primary focus for all major decisions.

The style of Servant-Leadership requires the president to be present and that he/she look, listen, think, discuss, evaluate, discern, and then decide with full realization that, consultation notwithstanding, the buck still stops on the president's desk. This leadership style takes enormous patience, time and energy, but I was comfortable with it because my constituents, colleagues, and board of trustees knew my philosophy, and it was a good fit for Fontbonne from 1995 to 2014.

The father of servant-leadership was the marvelous Robert K. Greenleaf (1904-1990). In *Ten Characteristics of the Servant Leader* (1998, pp. 3-6), author Larry Spears, reminds us servant-leadership requires a unified, continuous, and ethical approach to leadership based upon, "listening, empathy, healing, awareness, persuasion, conceptualization, foresight, stewardship, commitment to the growth of people, and building community." In my opinion, this is the essence of the social cement that can bind and strengthen any university. Further progress can be made by reading and utilizing the enormous wisdom contained in the book titled, *Leadership Is An Art*, by Max De Pree.

My leadership style also included the following components:

First, what I call the Five M's of Catholic higher education: mission, ministry, management, mystery (the sacraments), and yes, the indefatigable sine qua non of all institutions of higher education, money.

Second, an essential driver and reason why I recommitted my efforts every day was because of what Dr. Warren Bryan Martin called, "a Conspiracy of Conscience," where university resources are geared to balancing humanism and technology. (College Management, July 1972, vol. 7. n. 7, p. 2)

Third, I was also deeply motivated by the late and great president emeritus of Morehouse College, Dr. Benjamin E. Mays, who urged a spirit of restlessness and dissatisfaction with bigotry, racism, ignorance, greed, sickness (of self and soul), etc. Dr. Mays called this, Divine Discontent. He also admonished others to never "settle" or "surrender" because once that happens, one loses the will to carry on. ("Education Is" (Going to College Handbook), 1967 v. 30, p. 3)

God was teaching me that what we do is less important then why we do it because the "why" leads to motivation and that makes all the difference. I implemented this principle by putting students first, making decisions in a mode of discernment, and utilizing a philosophy of servant-leadership because presidents do not "run" the university. To the contrary, they should share the running of the university with the faculty and others via shared governance and not through top-down mandates which have a very short shelf life as has been the case with far too many failed presidencies.

Scripture Passages:

> In Philippians 2:5-8, who is doing the good work in you?
> Philippians 2:15-17 warns there are those who do things with wrong _____.
> What kind of fruit might this type of teacher produce?
> What kind of teacher are you called to be?
> Why?

Golden Nugget:

All people are caught up in doing the "what." Fewer people are committed to the "why" of the doing, but it is the "why" that makes all the difference.

-18-

REALIZE

As stated previously, my best answer as to "how and why" college and university presidents do what they do and should do is based upon my belief in servant leadership. University presidents must function in accordance with the specific mission of their institution, they serve at the pleasure of the board, and everything that they do and should do is subject to the court of public opinion.

The following realizations were gleaned from my nearly twenty years as a president, from experiences of my professional colleagues, and from other sources that I cannot accurately recall, but from which I learned valuable lessons.

- The president does not have a job; it is a 24/7/365 vocation.
- The president does not have an "off" switch; thus, this vocation is not for the faint of heart.
- The president must be a critical thinker, ethical leader, and charitable person.

- The president must be a visionary with the courage to make unpopular, but necessary, decisions.
- The president cannot mistake activity for accomplishment.
- The president cannot make side deals or take shortcuts.
- The president must be trustworthy, truthful, and transparent at all times.
- The president must have extraordinary intellectual, and emotional, psychological, physical, interpersonal, and spiritual stamina.
- The president must implement policy in a patient and persistent manner.
- The president must confer, communicate, and collaborate because the university is not a top-down organization.
- The president must acknowledge and support a campus culture of interdependence and shared governance.
- The president must understand that in decision making, it is better to think four times, hear three times, speak twice, and decide once.
- The president must be aware that his/her decisions are their "sermons," as well evidence of their true beliefs, and that they will be judged accordingly.
- The president must proclaim the academic mission (the formal curriculum) is preeminent, while also understanding the out-of-class experiences (the formative curriculum) are an equally vital and compelling part of the overall educational process.
- The president must understand that the tone is set at the top, and that accountability can be assigned, but responsibility cannot.
- The president should trust, but always verify.
- The president must know that everything has a price except one's character, integrity, and reputation, each of which are priceless.

- The president discovers that leadership is an art, and servant-leadership is a key to success.
- The president must realize that the primary reason for the existence of the university is the individual student, so they must always be kept at the center of the decision-making process.
- The president must recognize the enormous pressures and high stress in this vocation, so it is imperative to keep a balance of faith, family, friends, and fun in his/her life.
- The president must step away and not interfere once his/her successor's term of service begins.

Although it has turned out this way, "Realize" was not initially meant to include a brief course in higher education administration. Rather, the purpose was to give the reader some insight into lessons learned from my prior vocation as a university president. What I learned along the way was that I could never meet the required standards of the presidency absent prayer, and the deep belief that I was being guided by my Lord and Savior Jesus Christ. As St. Francis said, "Preach always and sometimes use words."

Scripture Passage:

> In Titus 2:1-8, the Apostle Paul teaches some basic foundations of discipleship.
> List the key passages and points that are most relevant to you at this time in your life.
> How will you implement these key principles in your life?

Golden Nugget:

Now that I am retired, I want to use the remainder of the time God has granted me as positively and productively as possible. Thus, I have chosen to write and share my faith journey, and even if only one person benefits, it is worth it. It is not only worth the time and effort; it is priceless!

-19-

SAUDI STUDENTS: MORAL DILEMMA

During the last few years of my presidency at Fontbonne University, we had a significant increase in the number of Saudi students. Some came from very wealthy backgrounds, most did not. Some were married with children, most were single men. Most were very conscientious students, some were not, and that was no different than for other groups of students, be they international or domestic. What was different with most, if not all, of the Saudi students was their keen political awareness and religious devotion. During my discussions with them, I would try to see the world through their political perspective and their religious convictions. We had a few minor differences of opinion, but we always respected each other and remained friends.

During the 2013-2014 academic year, my final year at Fontbonne, the president of the Saudi Student Organization asked if they could celebrate National Saudi Day, and I willingly said, "Yes." The students did a fine job planning the events, which included welcomes, the Saudi national anthem, food, music, photos, displays, and two guest speakers.

The first guest speaker gave a very interesting presentation regarding the discovery of oil in Saudi Arabia, with specific reference to Dammam No.7, the first commercial oil well in Saudi as of March 4, 1938. This came as an outgrowth of efforts by the late, King Abdulaziz Al-Saud, the founder of modern Saudi Arabia. Everyone in the audience, this writer included, praised the speaker for a job very well done.

Then the second speaker began by complimenting the Saudi students for organizing such a fine celebration to honor their country's founding as a modern day kingdom 1932. He also commended the Saudi students for their commitment to higher education and their multiple accomplishments during their time on campus. Then, with thoughtful intensity, he predicted that when they return home to Saudi Araba, they needed to be ready to face a moral dilemma.

Once the words "moral dilemma" were spoken, a great silence came over the entire audience. It became so quiet that you could almost hear a pin drop. The speaker than predicted that almost immediately upon their return to Saudi soil, they would be asked by many, possibly including those with extremist views, what it was really like to have lived and studied in the USA with the "infidels."

So, their moral dilemma would then become to either tell the truth or not. If after being in America and at Fontbonne, they had good reason to dislike, distrust, and even hate America, they should say it. If, however, they had grown to like, trust, and/or love America, they should say it. Either way, they would have to live with their answer for the rest of their lives. In today's world, they needed to be ready to address the reality of the inevitable questioning.

In order to "ease the tension" just a bit, the speaker then asked them to remember the warm hospitality and help they had received from the staff in the International Affairs Office, from the president and his wife during receptions in their home, and from the entire campus community. Then I, the second speaker, concluded my comments by telling them that I loved them.

I then took a deep breath as I stepped away from the microphone and podium and sat down. The silence was broken with loud and prolonged applause which brought tears to my eyes.

Scripture Passages:

Ephesians 4:15 says we are to speak the _____ in love.
What does this mean to you personally?
Does it create a moral dilemma for you?
Why or why not?

Golden Nugget:

Sometime you feel compelled to speak out, though not to chastise, criticize or condemn, but to call to the attention of others what they will be facing because of very predicable circumstances. This type of predictable moral dilemma affects our relationship with God and others. It is both secular and sectarian, and it is very real in the lives of people that I love.

-20-

PRESIDENT JAMES EARL "JIMMY" CARTER JR.

One day Monica and I received a very special invitation from our good friend and outstanding KMOX St. Louis radio show host, Charlie Brennan. It was an invitation to be in the audience when he hosted the thirty-ninth President of the Unites States, Mr. Jimmy Carter, who would be talking about the Camp David Peace Accords and his book titled, *We Can have Peace in the Holy Land.*

When Monica and I arrived at the radio station, we were startled to learn that the entire audience consisted of just the two of us and Charlie in the broadcast booth with President Carter. He was extremely gracious to Monica and thanked me for my service in the US Marine Corps and for dedicating my life to higher education. Just then, the warning sign flashed, and a few seconds later, Charlie and President Carter were on the live broadcast.

As President Carter said during the broadcast, following twelve days of negotiations, the Camp David Peace Accords were signed by Egyptian

President Anwar al-Sadat and Israeli Prime Minister Menachem Begin on September 17, 1978. This also led to the 1978 Nobel Peace Prize being awarded to both Sadat and Begin.

What most of history and the KMOX broadcast did not show was another fascinating and very personal feature of that peace process. During one of the advertising breaks, I asked President Carter, if during the negotiations there was any one key to getting the two leaders to sign the Peace Accords. President Carter smiled warmly as he went back to the live broadcast, and said that there was no single key. I thought "story over," but I was wrong.

When the next commercial break came, President Carter leaned forward and said, "Dennis, there really was one key but it did not occur during the formal negotiations."

He then shared the story of the night before the signing. During that time, Mr. Begin had reservations as to whether or not he could sign because of multiple and differing political pressures within the Israeli government. As Prime Minister Begin was preparing to retire for his last night at Camp David, he thanked President Carter for all of his efforts to bring peace to the Holy Land, and he also asked President Carter for a small favor. His simple request was for President Carter to give him a signed photograph to remind him of President Carter's efforts, thereby helping him to keep the hope of peace alive when he returned to Israel. President Carter bade Prime Minister Begin good night with the assurance that he would give him the photo before the Prime Minister departed the following morning.

President Carter then returned to his quarters, called his staff in DC, and instructed them to secure as many photographs as necessary for all of Mr. Begin's immediate family and close relatives. Those photos arrived at Camp David and Mr. Carter personally signed every one of them.

At the appointed time, Mr. Carter arrived at Mr. Begin's cabin, knocked on the door, and said that all of the transportation arrangements were ready for Mr. Begin's return home. President Carter then told us that Mr. Begin's suitcase was open on the bed, and Mr. Begin politely asked if President Carter had brought the photo. President Carter responded affirmatively and gave him the photos. Mr. Begin was surprised, and extremely appreciative.

President Carter said that Mr. Begin then looked at him with the realization that unless the Israeli and Egyptian Peace Accords were signed, the duty would fall to the next generation. President Carter said that he nodded affirmatively, and then Mr. Begin said, "I will sign," and that's exactly what he did.

President Carter then looked directly at me and said, "Dennis, that was the key."

To which I responded, "Thank you, Mr. President."

Without that very personal key, the Peace Accords would never have been signed. I thought, *What a wonderful coincidence.* Then, I once again remembered what Saint John Paul II said, "In matters of importance and consequence, there is no such thing as a mere coincidence, it is all part of God's plan." In addition, President Carter didn't have to share that story, but I'm thankful that he did because it helped me in my decision-making process as a university president.

Scripture Passages:

What did Jesus say in Matthew 5:9 about peacemakers?

What are these peacemakers going to be called?

Are you called to be a peacemaker?

How will you fulfill that call?

Golden Nugget:

We are all part of the human family. Now, more than ever, it is absolutely necessary to seek and secure local, regional, national, and international peace. To do less is not acceptable because those who want to limit or destroy our Constitutional freedoms and responsibilities are relentless. We can be no less relentless in our moral resolve and wisdom. It is far better than being engaged in ceaseless commitments to weapons and war.

PASSAGE 6

ALLOW GOD TO SPEAK
THROUGH YOU

-21-

GLAD DISTINCTIONS

A review of my overall academic record would show that I was a hard-working C+ student in high school and college. That was not the level of scholastic achievement that would lead anyone, including me, to believe that someday I would become a university president. I developed a love of learning, and once I got into graduate school, I earned B+'s and A's. Thank God, I wasn't tracked out early. Perhaps this can happen only in America.

At one time, I thought that I might become a middle school or a high school teacher, but my collegiate student teaching experience led me otherwise. Once I had my first administrative opportunity in higher education, I immediately knew administration was my calling and my profession to which I could give 100 percent every single day. On those days when I didn't meet that high standard, I was still thankful and joyful.

I have read countless books about the meaning of higher education, but few writers, if any, penned it better than, John Masefield, the poet laureate of England (1930-1967), who wrote:

*There are few earthly things more **splendid** then a university. In the days of broken frontiers and collapsing values... when every future looks somewhat grim... where ever a university stands, it stands and shines...*

*There are few things more **beautiful** than a university. It's a place where those who hate ignorance may strive to know, where those who perceive truth may strive to make others see, where seekers and learners alike bond together in the search for knowledge, and will honor thought in all its finer ways.*

*There are a few earthly things more **enduring** then a university. Religions may split into sect or heresy, dynasties may perish or be supplanted, but for century after century, the university will continue, and the stream of life will pass through it, and the thinker and the seeker will be bound together in the undying cause of bringing thought to the world.*

To be a member of one of those great societies must even be a "glad distinction."

I was truly blessed to have had a splendid, beautiful, and enduring vocation in university life. As an administrator at one college and four universities, it was truly a *glad distinction* and I wouldn't trade it for anything.

I was taught, primarily by the Jesuits, that I had an obligation to use my education for the greatest possible good, and to encourage others to do the same. My core belief was that we are all in need of redemption, and one of the best pathways to redemption is through the education of all of God's people, regardless of their socio-economic status, race, creed, color, national origin, gender or sexual orientation. The better educated people are, the better their chances are to keep hope alive, and to see justice and peace prevail in a world in need.

As a Christian and an American citizen, I believe that God was encouraging me to help others understand and value our Declaration of Independence, Constitution, Bill of Rights, and the Pledge of Allegiance. I wanted them to understand that we live in a republic not a democracy and that freedom is not free. The process of doing this was the gladdest distinction that I had as a president, especially when I shared these convictions with the students.

Scripture Passages:

> Proverbs 1:1-7 gives what advice to serious students?
>
> How are we to attain wisdom?
>
> Are you using what is available to you to attain wisdom, understanding, and discipline?

Golden Nugget:

During WWII Hitler bombed London relentlessly, but he did not bomb Oxford and Cambridge because if he prevailed, and thank God he didn't, he wanted those two world famous universities in their totality. In today's world, in many countries, young girls and women are not allowed to be educated. I believe the so called strong men and terrorist leaders are fearful that if women are educated they will fulfill their destiny, bring peace to the world, and those who reign will no longer have power over women by law or by force. So for me, it is the splendid, beautiful, and enduring nature of the university that inspires me and is the key to providing all of God's people, with the glad distinction of a university education.

-22-

THE DEAR NEIGHBOR

The Congregation of the Sisters of Saint Joseph (CSJ) dates back to 1650 in France. At that time, a group of women who wanted to take religious vows, worked with a Jesuit priest named Fr. Jean Paul Medaille S.J. It was Fr. Medaille who sought and received permission from the Pope to establish the first non-cloistered congregation of Catholic religious women, the Sisters of St. Joseph, who were dedicated to "divide the city" of Le Puy-en-Velay, and to do all the good that women are capable of doing for the "dear neighbor without distinction."

In 1832, six sisters sailed across the Atlantic Ocean, never again to return to France. They eventually settled in Carondelet, Missouri, which is very close to St. Louis. From that small start, the Congregation of the Sisters of St. Joseph of Carondelet has grown with their worldwide commitments to bring the gospel message of Jesus to all people, especially those most in need. It would take volumes for me to write about the compassion, courage, and competency of the CSJ's, and that has already been done by far better writers than I.

I want to emphasize that the charism includes to all dear neighbors without distinction regardless of their race, creed, culture, national origin, sexual orientation, etc. Their charism is full, complete, respectful, and accepting of all of God's people. During my years as servant-leader president of Fontbonne University, I tried to live according to the principles of the dear neighbor without distinction. Looking back, I hope this was evident via such things as our dedicated semester program, all-campus meetings, work with the Special School District, international education, outreach by our dedicated faculty to St. Louis, as well as statewide and internationally, campus, community church relationships, our special inter-institutional relationship with our close neighbors at Concordia Lutheran Seminary, and my cherished friendship with their distinguished president, Rev. Dr. Dale A. Meyer.

I felt so strongly about the essence of the dear neighbor without distinction, and the charism of the Sisters of Saint Joseph of Carondelet that I applied for, was accepted to, and completed the formation program to become an ACSSJ, Associate of the Congregation of the Sisters of Saint Joseph. I try to live my life accordingly.

God was giving me the "why" that was the basis for the "what, when, where, and how" of the decision-making process. Initiatives were implemented via careful analysis and review. I learned that to function properly as a president you must know, understand, and support the charism of the founders and sponsors of your university and with the best interests of the students at the heart of every decision.

Scripture Passage:

When Jesus was asked what the greatest commandment in the Law was in Matthew 22:36-40, what did He reply?

What does Jesus say is the second greatest commandment?

In Luke 10:29-37, who does Jesus say is your neighbor?

Golden Nugget:

The president should model and manifest the "dear neighbor without distinction" philosophy because he/she is not only "in" the university; he/she is "of" the university. And to many, he/she "is" the university.

-23 –

FAITH-BASED INTERPERSONAL RELATIONSHIPS

The people of God and, it is hoped, all of God's people have the desire to be acknowledged, assisted, accepted, appreciated, respected, celebrated, liked, and loved. We know, however, that this is not always what happens. Too often people are marginalized, misunderstood, and mistreated even in the world of higher education.

I knew that as a university president I needed guidelines or an operational philosophy for my dealings with multiple constituencies, including but not limited to: trustees, regents, Sisters of Saint Joseph of Carondelet, students, faculty, staff, administrators, alumni, benefactors, church leaders (especially the three archbishops with whom I worked (1995-2014), civic groups, neighbors (both residential and institutional), elected officials (local and state), inter-institutional colleagues, international colleagues, organizations (NCAA, NAACP, Urban League), multiple higher education groups (such as the Council for Independent Colleges and the Association of Catholic Colleges and Universities), Catholic Church affiliated organizations, state and federal government departments and agencies, accreditation agencies, media, etc. At any given time, one or more of these people or organizations expected my undivided attention and my very best efforts. When you are going at flank speed 24/7/365, it can become quite a challenge.

How did I do it? Ultimately it came down to a blend of three principles. First, a good friend and former Fontbonne University trustee, Bishop Paul Zipfel of Bismarck, North Dakota, once told my wife, Monica, and me that regardless of any differences, he always tries to "see the face of Christ" in every person with whom he is working. Frankly, I was stunned by the simplicity, power, and wisdom of Bishop Zipfel's philosophy, and I immediately tried to adopt it in both my personal and professional life.

Secondly, there was Mother Teresa, who said: "People are often unreasonable and self-centered. Forgive them anyway. If you are kind, people may accuse you of ulterior motives. Be kind anyway. If you are honest, people may cheat you. Be honest anyway. If you find happiness, people may be jealous. Be happy anyway. The good you do today may be forgotten tomorrow. Do good anyway. Give the world the best you have, and it may never be enough. Give your best anyway. For, you see, in the end, it is between you and God. It never was between you and them anyway."

The philosophical trilogy became complete when my dear friend Donna M. Carroll, President of Dominican University in River Forest, Illinois, reminded me that what university presidents do is "absorb chaos, give back calm, and provide hope." In this 21st century world of need, I found Donna's insights to be memorable, meaningful, and helpful.

I tried to integrate the faith-based lessons learned from Bishop Zipfel, Mother Teresa, and Donna Carroll into my operational DNA. There was a particular time, however, when I failed to do so. As matter of record, and for good reason, I lost both my patience and temper for about five minutes with a senior administrator. This resulted in an official investigation of my actions, plus strict guidelines for future interaction, which were carefully followed. That administrator voluntarily left the university a year later.

I share this information because no matter how hard you try to foster faith-based interpersonal relationships in the work environment, difficult personnel situations may develop nevertheless. Should that happen, avoid conflict and complications by literally "stepping away," and immediately seek legal counsel before going any further. Ultimately, justice is at the heart of faith-based interpersonal relations, and even in this case, justice prevailed.

Scripture Passage:

> Colossians 3:23 says we should work as if _____.
> Why do you think that principle is important in your dealings with others?
> Is this going to change the way you handle interpersonal relationships?

Golden Nugget:

I learned to prepare before the moment of "engagement." In your preparation, know how you will function philosophically, emotionally, legally, and spiritually, and then trust the process.

-24-

RABBI CARNEY ROSE: B'NAI AMOONA SYNAGOGUE

A person that I respect and admire is Rabbi Carney Rose. I was honored when he invited me to speak to the adult education members of his B'Nai Amoona congregation in Creve Coeur, Missouri. Truthfully, I became more scared than honored when he told me that the topic was to explain Catholicism to the attendees. I thought, "Wow, is that all?" Carney smiled, I smiled back, and then said something like, "I'm not a theologian, but I'll give it my best shot." What a profound response.

Well, I worked harder to prepare for that presentation than I had on any other presentation in my entire career. I not only didn't feel qualified, I was fearful of saying the wrong thing, especially since I was the president of a Catholic university. Regardless of my apprehension, I took it to prayer, did my research, and organized the presentation. I was then ready to go—almost.

On the morning of the presentation, I woke up with a headache, stomach cramps, and pains in my joints. At first, I thought it was psychosomatic and tried to block it out. But as the day went on, I got progressively worse–it was the real thing. At that time, Monica was out of town; when I picked her up in the late afternoon at Lambert Airport, my beloved wife and RN immediately realized that I was sick and urged me to call Rabbi Rose to postpone the presentation. We had a contest of wills because she was so concerned about my medical status and I was concerned about fulfilling my commitment. We both calmed down and when we got home, I wrapped myself in a blanket and shivered away until it was time to drive to B'Nai Amoona. I was on a mission.

As soon as we arrived at B'Nai Amoona, Rabbi Rose's reaction was the same as Monica's. He offered to postpone the presentation. I expressed my appreciation for the offer, but declined because it was a cold winter night and people were already arriving. Moreover, adrenaline had kicked in and I was ready to give it my best effort.

Rabbi Rose and the full house of attendees gave Monica and me a very warm welcome. Then, I began to speak about the Jewish Bible, which Christians and others refer to as the Old Testament. Then, I spoke about the New Testament, The Acts of the Apostles, and The Apostle's Creed, which took nearly forty-five minutes, so we took a scheduled break.

During the second part of the presentation, I spoke about the organizational structure of the Catholic church, the Seven Sacraments, the gift of faith, the importance of the words "I believe," and my personal efforts to be a live witness and disciple in accordance with the teachings of the Catholic faith. The audience was deeply respectful and very attentive. By this time, however, I was running out of energy, so Rabbi Rose said that it was time for closing questions and answers.

The Q & A was good and went on for about fifteen minutes. Then, Carney said there would be just two more questions. I can't remember the second to the last question, but I will never forget the last question.

A lovely woman asked, "If a woman cannot be a priest, monsignor, bishop, cardinal, or pope, then what was the highest thing that a woman can aspire to in the Catholic Church?"

I thought, "Wow! What a question!" I then looked in Monica's direction, she smiled warmly and offered a silent, "Good luck." When I glanced at Carney he rolled his eyes, and readjusted his yarmulke as if to also say, "Good luck." I gazed upward with my silent plea, "Jesus, please help me."

As soon as I did that, I became completely calm and the answer was clear.

So, I looked kindly into the woman's eyes and said, "In the Catholic church, women aspire to exactly the same thing that men do. It has nothing to do with organizational titles because what both women and men aspire to is sainthood."

She then looked directly at me and said, "Thank you. I understand."

Presentation over. Immediately thereafter, both Monica and Rabbi Rose asked me how I ever came up with that answer. I said that I prayed to Jesus and then the response, which is true, became self-evident in the context of the Catholic Christian tradition.

This was a wonderful example of the value and of inter-religious trust and respect, plus the opportunity to gain mutual understanding. Yes, I was sick with the flu for two days thereafter, but I was deeply thankful for all of God's blessings.

In Matthew 10:19-20, Jesus told His followers not to be worried about what to say when they were confronted about their faith because God's Spirit would put the words into their mouths.

> Have you ever found yourself in a position of trying to explain your faith, but were at a loss for words?
>
> How will you handle this the next time it happens?

Golden Nugget:

I realized I could not sufficiently explain Catholicism to this wonderful audience, but I learned that by giving a truly honest effort, it was well received. I also realized that by seeking the help of Jesus in the synagogue, my prayer was answered and I believe that it was for the greatest possible good under the given circumstances.

SIGNIFICANT RELATIONSHIPS

-25-

MONICA

Since Memorial Day, May 31, 1957, Monica and I have "been together" but not exactly in the way that phrase is commonly used in the 21st century. When we met, we were both fifteen years young and sophomores in high school. We were married in 1964, and I am beyond blessed to have had her as my wife for over fifty years. Since I am a Christian under construction and a sinner in need of redemption, if I ever gain eternal salvation, it will, in great part, be because of Monica's prayers and unconditional love for me, even when I didn't really deserve it. Bottom line, she is the love of my life.

May 31, 1957, was a beautiful sunny day. It was also expected to be a fun day. My all boy's Catholic high school was scheduled to take a Memorial Day boat ride with the girls from St. Agnes High School. The boat ride went from Battery Park in lower Manhattan, up the East River into Long Island Sound, and on to Rye Beach Amusement Park.

Upon arrival at the subway in Flushing, Long Island, a few of us sought directions from a group of girls who said they were going on the boat ride.

They knew the subway system better, so off we went together. We got to the departure site on time and before we knew it, we were under way. Shortly thereafter, our principal Bro. John Donoghue, CSC, got on the loud speaker and informed us that the girls from St. Agnes could not make the trip because their principal had decided to have school on Memorial Day to make up for a winter snow day. I turned to the girl next to me and she informed me that she did not attend St. Agnes. She was a student at Dominican Academy. Her name was, Monica Lennon. I liked her immediately. During both high school and college, we dated, but not exclusively. Both before and throughout our marriage, we shared joy and sorrow, victory and defeat, sickness and health, good times and bad, and somehow we always knew we would be together.

For years, Monica was akin to being a single parent because of the enormous amounts of time as an officer, graduate student, teacher, football player, coach, dean, vice president, president, etc., required of me. This encompasses a wide range of home addresses in Virginia, North Carolina, Massachusetts, Pennsylvania, Kentucky, Missouri, California, and now retirement back in North Carolina. We "served together" in the U.S. Marine Corps and at five different institutions of higher education: The College of the Holy Cross, Framingham State College, Duquesne University, University of Louisville, and Fontbonne University. We are blessed to have three children and nine grandchildren. More than ever before, we are aware that time moves swiftly and in only one direction. We have also been blessed to have an enormous number of loyal and loving friends.

In addition, we have countless good and great times, but those didn't necessarily strengthen our faith as much as times of stress. So, I will tell you about three times I came close to losing Monica. Each time, we came out of it stronger and more in love than ever before.

The first time I almost lost Monica was in the winter of 1965, and she was not even with me. We were in our early twenties, and she was nearly seven months pregnant with our first child, Patrick. I got a change of orders from Camp Lejeune, North Carolina, to the US Marine Corps Recruit Depot in California. Monica wanted to drive across the country with me, but I insisted she stay with her family in New York City and deliver the baby at St. Albans Naval Hospital.

On the second day of my trip to California, I was driving seventy miles per hour on Route 66, heading west across Oklahoma, when a driver ran a stop sign and crashed directly into the right front side of my car. The car was completely destroyed. Had Monica been with me, there was a 95 percent chance that she and the baby would have been killed. I was lucky to escape without serious injury.

The second time I almost lost Monica was in the 1980s, when I was working as VP for Student Affairs at Duquesne University. Even a quick review of history clearly shows that this was a period of significant trauma at Duquesne. This was especially true at the senior administrative levels, which brought the entire university to the brink of disaster. In addition, there were extremely serious criminal allegations regarding the behavior of four male varsity basketball players. This led to relentless media coverage, a prolonged criminal trial, findings of not guilty as charged, and then my personal and professional responsibility as VP for Student Affairs to review and decide the four cases within the rules and regulations of the student code of conduct, which I did.

This was a very difficult period of time, and although they were not criminally convicted, I found them to be in serious violation of university rules and regulations, and I sanctioned them accordingly. The end result was that both the *Pittsburgh Post-Gazette* and the *Pittsburgh Press* agreed that "Duquesne Stands Tall." Thus, almost a year after the original allegations, it was finally over.

What was not over, however, was the ongoing institutional tension, suffering and personal toll that it took on many people, this writer included. The truth be known, my professional conduct was acceptable and many said highly commendable. At other times, however, my personal conduct did not meet that standard. Specifically, I had distanced myself from Monica and drew closer to others, ultimately becoming both confused and conflicted.

Monica deserves enormous credit, because during that era of discontent, I was in serious danger of losing her, but her parents named her well. As St. Monica prayed for her son, St. Augustine, Monica prayed for me. Anyone who has read the Confessions of St. Augustine gets some idea as to how he fell from grace. At that time in my life, I was acting more like the pre-converted Augustine than St. Augustine.

The third time I almost lost Monica was in the 1990s, when she was diagnosed with breast cancer and eventually had a bilateral mastectomy. Through prayer and extraordinary medical care at Barnes Jewish Hospital in St. Louis, Monica made a full recovery and, thank God, is still with me. As of July 1, 2014, we retired to Huntersville, NC, and I love her more deeply and dearly now than at any other time in my life.

Now that I have celebrated my 73rd birthday, I am convinced more than ever that my meeting Monica when we were teenagers was truly part of God's plan. *I am still a Christian under construction in need of redemption.* To that end I try to be a good husband, father, grandfather, citizen, friend, and live according to the gospel message of Jesus. To the degree that I succeed, I do so with humility, and to the degree that I fall, I vow to get back up and try to be a witness to the Gospel message.

A key lesson we learned is that to really function effectively, efficiently, and ethically in life, we must be congruent professionally and personally.

Scripture Passages:

> How does Ephesians 5:28 describe the love of a husband for his wife?
> How does Proverbs 31:12 describe a wife?
> Are you the spouse God has called you to be?
> Are there things you need to do differently to honor the gift God has given you in your spouse?

Golden Nugget:

Stress and pressure are not acceptable reasons for acting improperly with your spouse. Do not compromise, do not drift, and do not do anything except love your one true love, your partner for life if you are fortunate enough to have one.

-26-

EIWP-GP

While I was the Vice President for Student Affairs at Duquesne University in the early to mid-1980s, I was blessed to have two very special friends, Ed and Mari Etta Stoner. Ed was a distinguished labor lawyer for Reed Smith in Pittsburgh, and Mari Etta was a Ph.D. consulting psychologist.

Ed was also outside legal counsel for Duquesne and we worked together on many important university legal matters. In later years, he became the outstanding president of the National Association of College and University Attorneys. Like Ed, Mari Etta was specially gifted, and she always went above and beyond while she was helping people solve their hardest and most complex problems.

One evening, Ed and Mari Etta hosted a dinner party at their home. Monica and I were among the six invited guests. During the course of the evening, Mari Etta received three phone calls. Since this was prior to cell phones, she did not have sufficient distance or privacy, and we couldn't help but realize that something serious was happening. The first two calls were intense and included professional "give and take" between Mari Etta and a colleague as how best to resolve the problem. We minded our business; no one asked her anything.

When she was serving dessert, the phone rang again but this time things were different. Evidently something very good had happened because Mari Etta had an expression of enormous relief. She said to the caller that she would follow up first thing the next morning.

Upon concluding that third phone call, she looked at Ed and said, "EIWP-GP."

Ed smiled knowingly and said, "Exactly."

The rest of us looked at each other wondering what Mari Etta and Ed were talking about.

Finally one of us said, "We don't want to overstep our bounds. We realize that you were dealing with a difficult situation which appears to be at least temporarily under control."

Mari Etta nodded affirmatively.

Then the question was asked, "So, what does EIWP-GP mean?"

Mari Etta glanced at Ed and they both smiled. Then she said, "EIWP-GP means Everything Is Working Perfectly–God's Plan, not our plan."

We all looked at each other and realized that we had just been given a powerful and summative faith-based life lesson that we could and should carry forward. That is exactly what I have done.

With Mari Etta's permission, I had business-size cards printed that explain the meaning of the letters EIWP-GP and distribute them frequently. Most people are deeply appreciative. While serving at the University of Louisville, my Kentucky license plate displayed EIWP-GP. I still had that license plate on my car when I became president of Fontbonne, where I was once reminded by one of our most distinguished faculty members, Dr. Mary Abkemeier that in my case EIWP does not stand for Expert in Word Processing. How right she is.

I have used the philosophy of EIWP-GP for over thirty years. It has helped me an inestimable number of times to accept, appreciate, and adjust to life as it comes, especially if I don't understand it. Succinctly stated, it means I endeavor to trust and abide by God's plan.

It was no mere coincidence that Mari Etta and Ed Stoner taught me about EWIP-GP. Through Mari Etta and Ed, God was teaching me to be aware, awake, and affirming to His call. Over the years, when things went well, I thanked God, and when I thought they didn't go well, I simply said, "It is just not part of God's plan," and I went on to other things with peace of mind.

For those who want more information, you can continue to learn from Mari Etta Stoner via her website www.everythingisworkingperfectly.com. Mari Etta writes, "Everything Is Working Perfectly according to an incredible divine plan allowing us to receive exactly what we need, at exactly the right time to accomplish it. We draw people and experiences into our lives to help us to learn about love and how to love unconditionally. These interactions are not always positive, but they are always perfect."

Scripture Passage:

Read Romans 12:2.

What does this passage tell you about how to know God's perfect will and plan for your life?

How is EIWP-GP going to help you face difficulties and triumphs in life?

Golden Nugget:

EIWP-GP, along with an understanding that there are no mere coincidences, can bring a person greater trust, faith, and a deeper understanding of the Christian approach to life.

-27-

THE KEY DECISION

I was appointed president of Fontbonne College, now Fontbonne University in the fall of 1994. My first official day in office was scheduled for January 1, 1995, and I knew I had to hit the ground running. That required, among many other things, finishing my work at the University of Louisville and getting the right people on board at Fontbonne. I asked the assistant to the president if she was interested in staying, and then we could determine if it was the right working relationship or not. She thought about it and then declined, so a small advertisement was placed in the *St. Louis Post-Dispatch* for the position. This resulted in a few dozen applicants all of whom appeared to have the preferred qualifications and experience—all except one.

After sorting through the applications and CVs, I interviewed many candidates, all of whom were women, most of whom had held senior assistant positions with CEOs of major St. Louis corporations or not-for-profits—all except one. They all had the basic qualifications—all except the very last candidate. She did not have executive secretarial or executive assistant experience nor did she have a college degree.

She was a native of St. Louis, who had worked in a number of settings over the years, including a major law firm, assistant to the dean at Saint Louis University School of Dentistry, and as the assistant director of an early intervention center for infants and toddlers with special needs. She was married with two college-age daughters, and based upon her letter of interest and CV, I had a very positive feeling about this candidate. In addition I was keenly aware that this was the key personnel decision of my presidency, so it had to be right.

When Patricia Etter walked into the office for her interview and we started talking about the job requirements of the executive assistant to the president and board of trustees, I knew almost immediately, she was the absolute right person for the position. Her communication skills were excellent, her questions were spot on and her class, dignity, and relational skills were outstanding.

My first impressions about her love of people and academics were confirmed when she told me that when she graduated from Notre Dame High School in St. Louis, she had a full scholarship offer to attend Fontbonne, but she had chosen a different pathway.

Patricia and I worked together for nearly twenty years, and she was absolutely outstanding in the performance of her duties. She was always adaptable and the key communicator and liaison with the Board of Trustees, Council of Regents, Sisters of Saint Joseph of Carondelet, all campus constituents, benefactors, community and church leaders. Her value to all, including this former president, is priceless.

Over the years, Patricia, her husband, Tom, Monica and I became close friends, and we remain so today. She has my absolute trust and confidence in all matters because of her ability to make effective and ethical choices.

Patricia is now the executive assistant to the president and board of trustees for my successor Dr. J. Michael Pressimone. I am confident that she will continue to work for greatest possible good of Fontbonne.

God was teaching me to look beyond credentials and get to the essence of the person. I also learned that the institutional and interpersonal fit was non-negotiable regarding the president and the executive assistant. Finally, God was telling me to "trust my gut" in this vital and extremely important personnel appointment.

I prayed that Patricia would accept my offer, and she did so on Christmas Day, 1994. Patricia was the first person I hired during my career at Fontbonne. That decision was a magnificent way and a blessing to start such a special journey.

Scripture Passage:

> 1 Samuel 16:7 says God looks at things differently than man does. Explain this difference.
> How does knowing this change the way you look at others?

Golden Nugget:

> *People like Patricia are very rare so do not miss it when God brings someone special into your life. Understand that such a person is a constant blessing and do nothing to ever harm such a precious relationship.*

-28-

CHRISTMAS 2014

Christmas 2014 was my first in retirement. For the first time in decades, I was far less caught up in the commitments and commercialism of what has, unfortunately, come to be known as the holiday season. All too frequently this becomes a stress-filled season that does not seem to focus on the true meaning of Christmas, which of course, is the celebration of the birth of our Lord and Savior Jesus Christ.

So, during Christmas 2014, more than ever before, I had the desire to be with my immediate family and to communicate with some special friends who were and are in need, with the hope of providing just a little peace and joy on December 25.

God was telling me to remember the true meaning of Christmas and to share that with others. He was also telling me it all comes down to do you really do believe that Jesus Christ is the Savior of the world. If we really do believe that, then we must be ready to be a disciple of Christ, and if necessary, to suffer for our Christian faith.

Sooner or later, all of our lives will end, and then it all comes down to just you and God. That can be a really scary or a really joyous thought, depending upon how we live our lives. So, in my case, having lived over three score and thirteen, I have chosen to try to become more like the little children who accept and practice their faith. For as Jesus said, "Unless you become like little children, you will not enter the gates of heaven" (Matthew 18:3). Jesus was talking to His disciples. If we profess to be His followers and His disciples in this present age, we too must become like little children and come to Him in humble faith and trust.

Christmas 2014 was different for me, and I want to keep it that way.

Scripture Passages:

Read Psalm 23:1-6.
What are some of God's amazing promises given to you in this psalm?
What do you really believe?
Do your actions match up to what you say you believe?
Are there things you need to change in your life?

Golden Nugget:

We are not here to "be" Christians, we are here to "live" like Christians, and to do whatever we can to exemplify the essence of the words, "I believe."

USING WHAT WE HAVE BEEN GIVEN WISELY

-29-

THE HOLY LAND

During our time in St. Louis, Monica and I were invited to join the Northern Lieutenancy of the Equestrian Order of the Holy Sepulcher of Jerusalem. The EOHSJ aims to strengthen the members' practice of Christian life, with emphasis on fidelity to the Pope. The EOHSJ also emphasizes teaching of the Church, the principles of charity, to sustain the faith, and to increase the charitable cultural, social and institutions of the Catholic Church in the Holy Land, especially the sacred Christian places. The Order tries to help Christians in the Holy Land achieve educational and professional levels of competence, enabling them to fully participate on a level equal to those of other faiths.

Today, the Christian population in the Holy Land is only 2 to 3 percent of the Holy Land, so the type of commitment being made by the EOHSJ is extremely important. The EOHSJ expects members to be witnesses and disciples regarding the Gospel message of Jesus. In order to become more knowledgeable witnesses and disciples, members are strongly encouraged to make a pilgrimage to the Holy Land, which we did in 2008. That pilgrimage, with about thirty other EOHSJ members from the Midwest, far exceeded our expectations and deepened our faith immeasurably.

During the pilgrimage, we were security-cleared by the Israeli military and then we crossed over the border into the West Bank to visit Bethlehem. After praying at the birthplace of Jesus and other sacred sites, we traveled a short distance to Bethlehem University. BU, as it is referred to, was founded in 1973 per the request of Pope Paul VI. It should also be noted that BU is the first university in the West Bank. It is a co-educational with an enrollment of nearly 3,300 students of which 71 percent are Muslim and 29 percent are Christian. Women students outnumber the men three to one.

The university is very fortunate to be under the excellent leadership of the De LeSalle Christian Brothers. Moreover, BU operates in a distinctively Lasallian tradition. BU's gifted Vice Chancellor and CEO is Brother Peter Bray, FSC, Ed.D., who refers to BU as "an oasis of peace and a beacon of hope." How true I would find those words to be both during and after we concluded the pilgrimage.

Upon our return to St. Louis, I started to receive e-mails indicating that a Bethlehem University student named, Berlanty Azzam, had gone from Bethlehem University to Ramallah for a job interview. The Israeli military cleared her when she departed, but detained her upon her return claiming that she did not have the correct passport or papers. Berlanty is a Palestinian Christian, whose home is in Gaza. During her interrogation, she explained her documents were the only ones that she had and that they had been issued by the proper authorities. The Israeli military disagreed with her, so they drove her back to Gaza during a very dangerous time period. Subsequently, she endured and lost a legal battle in which she sought permission to return to BU.

She did, however, complete her academic requirements while in Gaza, and she received her BU undergraduate degree. Thereafter, she departed Gaza, entered Egypt, and found her way to the USA. To recount how all of this happened would require an entire book or film documentary, so I will not go into all of those details.

What I will say, however, is that through the EOHSJ, Monica and I unexpectedly met Berlanty in St. Louis. We both reached out to her and she enrolled in the graduate school at Fontbonne University. Because of the philanthropic generosity of many of our friends and associates, she earned her MBA in two years and had a positively significant experience both on campus and in the community. Berlanty is still in the United States, and I hope and pray that eventually the immigration laws will permit her to seek and secure American citizenship. If that happens, she will add to her already admirable legacy the fact that she has always been a woman of faith and a sterling example of Brother Peter's reference to Bethlehem University as a beacon of hope for so many deserving students.

I believe there is a reason everything happens, including Berlanty's saga. I have shared her story because we never know how life will unfold, but when it does we have to choose to either help or not. It is much better to provide the help especially to those most in need.

Scripture Passages:

2 Timothy 4:1-5 admonishes us to do what?

Why are we given this charge?

How are you going to fulfill it?

Golden Nugget:

I believe that all things have a purpose and are connected. I also believe that only God knows all of the connections. Thus, we will be judged by the scope and sincerity of our responses to whatever part of the purpose and connections come our way.

-30-

TIME

No matter who we are: male or female, young or old, tall or short, black or white, European or Asian, good or bad, sick or healthy, rich or poor, saint or sinner, we are each given only a certain amount of time on planet Earth. As the renowned author Ed Hayes stated, "We are all planetary pilgrims on spaceship Earth and we don't know when our individual journeys will end."

Paraphrasing, Michael Quist wrote that people constantly run after time either to try to "get" more time or to "fill" the time given with as much "doing" as possible. It seems that people continually rush toward and through time without really enjoying the journey. For example, the young are frequently inclined toward behavior that could described as "time urgency." They rush to become "of age" as soon as possible in order to engage in adult activities. The elders, with much more experience and wisdom, are inclined to be far less urgent and much more appreciative of whatever gift of time they still have.

After nearly half a century in higher education, I am convinced that most people, especially college/university students, do not have a deep understanding of their mortality or their vulnerability. I believe, therefore, that it is important for people to periodically slow down. This can provide the opportunity to reflect upon God's non-replenishable gift of time. Since time is both God given and limited, we should all do our absolute best to maximize this incredible gift.

In the Jewish Bible which Christians call the Old Testament, time is clearly proclaimed in The Book of Ecclesiastes (paraphrased):

> *For there is a time for every season under heaven,*
> *A time for war a time for peace,*
> *A time for planting, a time for uprooting what was planted,*
> *A time for joy, a time for sorrow,*
> *A time for embrace, and a time to refrain from embracing,*
> *A time to love and a time to hate,*
> *A time to be born and a time to die.*

As I entered my sixties and am now experiencing my seventies, I have almost become obsessed with the opportunities for the positive good that time provides. When I think about my final judgment under God (which in high school we referred to as JUG when we received disciplinary detention), I want to at least be able to say that I understood the precious gift of time and used it to the best of my ability which includes writing this book. I do so with the hope that at least my family and close friends will know that I tried to accomplish this in the spirit of Teddy Roosevelt's 1910 penning about it's not the critic who counts, "The credit belongs to the man in the arena...who strives valiantly; who errs, who comes up short again and again...who spends himself on a worthy cause...and who at the worst, if he fails, at least fails greatly, so his place shall never be with those cold and timid souls who know neither victory nor defeat."

So, regardless of one's state in life, we should all think deeply about time and what we are called to do with the time God has given us. God has alerted me to a sense of awareness and balanced urgency regarding the time I have been given.

I encourage others, especially university students, not to waste their time because habits formed regarding the effective, efficient, and ethical use of time are critical in order for a person to fulfill his/her God-given potential.

Scripture Passage:

> Reread Ecclesiastes 3:1-6.
> How are you being wise with the time you have been allotted in this life?
> How are you using your God-given talents?
> How is your life influencing those around you on a daily basis?

Golden Nugget:

Like Matthew's gospel about the use of our God-given talents, we must multiply them as much as possible with the time that God gives us.

-31-

THE DASH

T. E. Lawrence wrote, "All people dream, but not equally. Those who dream at night in the dark recesses of their minds wake up in the day to find it was vanity. But the dreamers of the day are dangerous people, for they may act upon their dreams with open eyes and make it possible." In order to actualize the potential of dreams, one must be thoughtful and insightful, concerning the realization that there is only a certain amount of time to accomplish it.

All of us are Alpha and Omega people with an unknown timeline between our birth and death. When that time has expired, most people are buried and their tombstones may or may not have a special message on them, but they will have the Alpha, the date of birth, and the Omega, the date of death. Between the two dates, one always finds "the little dash," and to me, that represents everything that a person has done throughout his/her entire life. When I look at a tombstone, therefore, I think about the person's allotted time. I think about what the person did in life, but also about how and why he or she did it. I think about how formidable and fragile life really is. I think about how we should all do the next right things, and about my own mortality.

Books have been written about this, but my purpose is simply to awaken my cerebral cortex, hopefully yours as well, to the reality of "the little dash," so that we can focus our time, energy, and efforts toward making this world the best possible place for all of God's children, from conception until we receive the call to come home.

If we awaken to the deeper meaning of "the little dash," we can, as T.E. Lawrence wrote, become dreamers of the day. By being evermore thankful, truthful, and transparent regarding all aspects of our lives, we will become ever closer to God and to the salvation messages contained in the Bible which I once heard referred to as *Basic Information Before Leaving Earth*.

To use a sports analogy, participants and spectators frequently hold up four fingers as they begin the fourth quarter of football games as a reminder that this is their final challenge and their last chance to win the game. So, in like manner, I hold up four fingers because I am now well into my personal fourth quarter, and I am fine with that. Finally, I hope and pray that the messages in this book will prove to be worthy of "the little dash" of my life by somehow helping others on their life's journey.

Scripture Passages:

Revelation 20:12-13, 21:3-4 speak about life after death.
Do you know where you will spend your eternity?
What will the "dash" on your tombstone represent?
What changes are you going to make so your "dash" makes significant change in your life and in others as well?

Golden Nugget:

Do not fall victim to the human fallacy that you may be the one and only person who lives forever (here on earth) and has no Omega.

SPEECHES, WORDS, AND SAYINGS

-32-

TWO SPEECHES: SPAIN AND TAIWAN

I am not a linguist. This can easily be proven by my consistent high school struggle with Latin and sometimes Spanish. That notwithstanding, when representing Fontbonne University in Europe and Asia, I was determined to address audiences in their native languages.

In the spring of 1997, Sr. Joan Lescinski, CSJ, Ph.D., Monica, and I arrived in Barcelona, Spain. At the time, Sr. Joan was Vice President and Dean of Academic Affairs at Fontbonne College now Fontbonne University. Currently, Sr. Joan is doing exceptionally well in her second presidency at St. Ambrose University, Davenport, Iowa.

We were warmly greeted, and I was invited by the president of the business college to participate in the upcoming commencement ceremony, which would be held in two days. The day before the commencement our guide from the college took us on a car ride to visit Monserrat. During the ride, I asked him to please critique what I intended to say at the next evening's commencement ceremony. As I was speaking, he winced, then cringed, so I asked him if my content was inappropriate. He reassured me the content was fine and encouraged me to keep speaking, which I did. However, I knew that something was still wrong, so I continued my efforts to find out. Finally, Pedro said that I was speaking Castilian, to which I agreed. Then, with extreme politeness but with explicit clarity, he told me that in Barcelona they speak Catalan not Castilian. So, I immediately started to change my speech, and the next night gave it in my best NYC/Catalan accent, which was evidently good enough because President Mas and the graduates all gave me a "well done" ovation as I finished my address.

A few years later, I tried the home language speech again. Only this time it was in Taipei City, Taiwan. The audience was comprised of distinguished faculty, administrators, graduates of both the National Taiwan University of Art and Fontbonne University, as well as friends of both institutions. Frankly, this speech in Mandarin was much more difficult to prepare for and deliver than the previous one in Barcelona.

My Chinese helpmate at Fontbonne consistently warned me to be very careful because with only the slightest variation in tone or accent, you accidently can change the entire meaning of what you intend to say and run the risk of confusing or insulting your audience. When the time came, I was very nervous and extremely careful not to make mistakes in elocution. I did this with, as they say, my heart on my sleeve because I had so much respect for these people, many of whom are still my close friends. As in Spain, my efforts and execution went very well, for which I gave great thanks to my helpmate in St. Louis.

The Barcelona trip happened because of Sister Joan. The Taipei trip happened because of the late and great Dr. Huang Chung "Jack" Liu, a former trustee of Fontbonne University. I am still close friends with Sr. Joan, with Dr. Liu's widow, Dr. Eva Salazar Liu, and with the Liu children,

Joshua, and Isabella, who is an excellent student, true leader, and honors graduate of Fontbonne.

I share these stories because, in this world in need, I am convinced that trying to communicate with people in their own language demonstrates respect. In turn, that respect has the potential to grow into mutual trust and understanding to enhance justice and peace.

Scripture Passages:

Read 1 Corinthians 12:31-13:13.
> This passage lists many ways we can serve God and others, but it also says if we do not have one very important thing, it will all be for nothing.
> What is that one important ingredient?
> Why is it so very important?

Golden Nugget:

I learned from firsthand experience that people around the world have much more in common with us than we realize. So, the aforementioned trust becomes much more than a social contract, it becomes a covenant based upon love which is ultimately the sine qua non or essential element that will prevail against the persecutions of the early 21ˢᵗ century radical extremism.

-33-

TENTH ANNIVERSARY OF 9/11

am proud to be a native of New York City. The first time radicals tried to destroy the Twin Towers in 1993, I was fifty-one years old and a member of the Middle States Accreditation Team for the John Jay College of Criminal Justice, which is located in mid-town Manhattan. I remember it like it was just yesterday. We were conducting the exit interview when an aide to the college president whispered something to him, and the president's expression became one of significant concern. He apologized to us and said that he had to leave immediately due to an emergency downtown. Shortly thereafter, we found out about the bombing at the Twin Towers.

Then, eight years later, it happened again, only this time it was much worse. Like most everyone else, I can remember exactly where I was on 9/11/01. In my case, after completing a workshop and consultation at the University of Wisconsin at Stevens Point on 9/10/11, I saw the TV broadcasts, then proceeded to drive back to Missouri. Perhaps unlike most everyone else, I can also remember exactly where I was ten years later on Sunday, 9/11/11, the tenth anniversary of 9/11.

During the week prior to September 11, 2011, I felt a deep unrest in my mind, heart, and soul. At the core of my unrest was my concern for the well-being of a number of my Muslim friends who are also American citizens, who practice their Islamic religion faithfully, and clearly are not militant extremists, but were being discriminated against emotionally, if not directly. So, my question became– what can I possibly do for them at the time of the tragic anniversary?

I decided to call Dr. Ghazala Hayat, M.D., a Muslim and distinguished member of the department of neurology and psychiatry at the Saint Louis University School of Medicine. Dr. Hayat is also a leader in the St. Louis Interfaith Partnership. So, I asked Dr. Hayat if it would be both possible and permissible for me to attend her Mosque, Daar-Ul-Islam, on Waldman Road in Manchester, Missouri. Although Dr. Hayat seemed pleased to receive my request, she wanted to know why I was seeking this permission. I told her I wanted to stand with her people as an American Christian who did not want to see innocent American Muslims be directly or indirectly blamed for 9/11. A few days later, I received permission to attend.

As I recall, there was an interim imam, and he warmly welcomed me to the Mosque, as did the many others with whom I interacted. When the day came, I could not walk without a cane because of a severe case of sciatica, so I decline his offer to prostrate during holy prayers.

Then, much to my amazement, as the prayers concluded. the presiding imam introduced me and invited me to address the faithful. I was shocked and completely unprepared, so I just turned it over to God and came forward. After thanking everyone for their warm welcome, I assured them that I was not going to preach. What I did do was ask for a show of hands indicating how many of those present were American citizens. I think every hand went up including mine. I then asked for a show of hands indicating how many present had nothing to do with 9/11, and the results were the same.

I stated that we all were fortunate to live in the United States of America and assured them that as a former Marine Corps officer, I would be honored to defend their constitutional freedoms and responsibilities. I the underscored that freedom is a very precious thing and that it is not free. Finally, I assured them that as the president of a Catholic university, I would stand with them against unwarranted and unjust discrimination related to 9/11. I urged that we try to work together against the extremists and jihadists, whose methods and motives are, at the very least, questionable and harmful, if not hateful. As I look back on it, I guess I did preach. The Spirit guided me to it and guided me through it. Shortly thereafter, we all had lunch together and I was very humbled and thankful that they appreciated the fact that I had reached out and wanted to be with them.

Much has happened since both 9/11/01 and 9/11/11. The world is much more radical and less safe. Consequently, we must also realize terror is effective only to the degree that people are afraid and unwilling to do everything necessary, and I mean everything, in order to prevail against the forces of intolerance and radical extremism.

Scripture Passages:

Read Romans 3:9-18.
  What wisdom have you gleaned from this chapter and this passage of scripture in regard to interfaith relationships?

Golden Nugget:

I firmly believe that the best, and perhaps the only antidote for radicalism is for people to establish real interfaith relationships. The basis of those relationships must be mutual trust and love. It will also take considerable time and relentless effort, but that may prove to be the only way we prevent a total crisis that ends up in an all-out religious war and the possible end to humankind as we know it.

-34-

SAINT LOUIS RAMS

In the late 1990s and early 2000s, I was invited by the Saint Louis Rams to speak to the rookies during the preseason training sessions. My assignment had nothing to do with Xs and Os, rather, it was focused upon certain realities and alerts that would help them become successful as members of the NFL, both on and off the playing field.

First, I tried to get those young men to realize that they were members of a very small and select minority group. Their membership in this special minority group was based upon their God-given athletic abilities. However, they also needed to realize that although they would have hard practice sessions, their stress paled in significance to that of other men and women of their age who were fighting in the military to preserve the very freedom that permitted these rookies to play professional football.

I also emphasized that they were now public figures whose behavior would be closely watched and judged by the media and others. Therefore, they had a duty and responsibility to not sully, in any way, the good name of the Saint Louis Rams. To the contrary, they had the opportunity and responsibility to exemplify the highest standards of personal and professional conduct, and they should do nothing less.

I warned them about gambling, drugs, sexual misconduct, drinking, etc. I did so with the full realization that these were young men who had already had numerous life experiences, were about to earn enormous sums of money, and already knew what it meant to be living on the edge. They were still mostly between twenty-one and twenty-three years of age with a lot to learn. I took the opportunity to give them a couple of alerts they could easily remember

I learned the first alert during a leadership conference in St. Louis years ago; thus, I want to give credit where credit is due; it goes to Mr. Byrd Baggett of New Hope, Alabama. In athletic terms, his question to the players was, *What does PGA stand for?* One or more of them quickly responded Professional Golf Association, to which I would agree. But as I learned at the leadership conference, it can also stand for Pride, Greed, and Arrogance. Thus, the alert and admonition was to stay humble, straight, and strong and to be very careful of the dangers of pride, greed, and arrogance especially since the average length of time for most NFL careers is only 3.3 years according to the NFL Players Association.

The second alert had to do with their competitive personalities. So I asked them when they lined up did they really believe that they were better than their opponents or not? They all said, "YES." I pointed out that their affirmative response went to their ego strength and that was both good and necessary if they ever expected to make it in the NFL.

I followed that up by writing the word "ego" on the board. Then right next to it I wrote it again "EGO" in BIG capital letters. I pointed out that both words are spelled the same and are pronounced the same, but they look different and they are very different in meaning. A balanced "ego" in all walks of life is good. But a big ego is fraught with danger because it can and frequently does mean Edging God Out. Once that happens, one's essential priorities get mixed up, performance usually declines, and then players are NFL (meaning Not For Long). I learned the "EGO" alert from the late and great, Robert "Bob" Brooks, of St. Louis, MO.

These presentations covered other things as well and usually took forty-five minutes to an hour. By the time I was finished, they were extremely focused and attentive because the PGA, EGO, and NFL messages were intentionally designed in order to awaken their cerebral cortexes and help them make the right type of decisions throughout their NFL careers. In like manner, I used the alerts to keep me properly focused as a university president.

Scripture Passages:

     P – Proverbs 16:18 says, _____

     G – Proverbs 15:27 says, _____

     A – Romans 11:20 says, _____

Golden Nugget:

Everyone must manage his or her ego. So, to be self-controlled and properly focused as a professional athlete, doctor, lawyer, business person, husband, wife, parent, teacher, entertainer, vowed religious leader, etc. is what should be happening if one really believes in the love of God, love of self, and love of others.

-35-

WORDS

In the late 1990s, I visited my good friend, Gerry Cassidy, Esq., in Washington, D.C. During my visit I noticed a book titled, *Words that Shook the World: 100 Years of Unforgettable Speeches and Events (2002)*, by Richard Greene, with Florie Brizel. Among the twenty speeches that shook the world one finds the following:

1903 Theodore Roosevelt, "You Cannot Improve on it. Leave it as it is" (Speech at the Grand Canyon).

1933 Franklin D. Roosevelt, "...The only thing we have to fear... is fear itself." (First Inaugural Address).

1939 Lou Gehrig, "The Luckiest Man on the Face of the Earth" (Farewell Speech)

1945 Douglas MacArthur, "The Entire World is Quietly at Peace," (Unconditional Surrender of Japan).

1945 Albert Einstein, "The war is won, but peace is not," (Nobel Prize Anniversary Dinner).

1948 Eleanor Roosevelt, "... the international Magna Carta of all men everywhere," (Statement of Adoption of Universal Declaration of Human Rights).

1963 Dr. Martin Luther King Jr., "I have a Dream" (March on Washington for, jobs and freedom).

1974 Barbara Jordan, "My faith in the Constitution is whole, it is complete, it is total." (House of Representatives on the Impeachment of President Nixon).

1993 Yitzhak Rabin, "Enough of blood and tears. Enough," (Signing of the Israeli-Palestinian Declaration of Principles).

1997 Princess Diana as remembered by Earl Spencer, "...the unique, the complex, the extraordinary and irreplaceable..." (Eulogy).

Then, much more recently, Christmas time 2014, while I was in Barnes and Noble Bookstore, another book shook me. The book is titled, *Rainbow in the Cloud: The wisdom and spirit of Maya Angelou*. I first met Ms. Angelou in the early 1990s through my dear and now deceased friend, Dr. Jim Scott (former VP of Student Affairs of Georgia State University and the University of Florida).

There are many words that shook me in, *Rainbow in the Cloud*, and I totally agree with Random House Publishers when they remind us that Maya said, "Words mean more then what is set down on paper" (book jacket). "I've learned that people will forget what you said, people will forget what you did, but people will never forget how you made them feel" (pg. 41).

Throughout my career, I learned that words, time, and place are very important. I also learned that how you make people feel is even more important. The authors of the previously mentioned speeches that shook the world, and Maya Angelou were all veterans in their respective areas. Compared to them, as a writer, the best that I can hope to be is a very humble beginner. As I learned, and continue to learn from their insights and wisdom, I looked for a few powerful words that can really affect how people feel. I can't remember the original source but I certainly do remember the eight such words:

Please,

Thank you,

Forgive me,

I love you.

I like these eight words because they are sterling examples of "meaning more then what is set down on paper."

I will focus on just two of them, "Forgive me," because of the eight these two are the most difficult to understand and actualize. Somewhere along the line, we have all had reason to say, "I'm sorry." But that is not the same thing as saying, "Forgive me."

To state that you are "sorry" is good, and it comes from you to the offender to the offended person. But to seek forgiveness means that the offended person must be engaged and willing to reconcile with you in order for both of you to heal your feelings, emotions, hearts, and souls. Essentially stated, forgiveness is a much higher standard than sorrow.

C.S. Lewis wrote, "To be a Christian means to forgive the inexcusable because God has forgiven the inexcusable in you." As we look around the world, instead of becoming ever closer to universal peace, we find ourselves on the brink of disaster because of racism, bigotry, ignorance, violations of human rights, economic disparity, disease, terrorism, religious persecution, warfare both cyber and human. Thus, we must work on the art of forgiveness and commit to doing everything possible to secure and enhance world peace.

God wanted me to realize the power and real meaning of words and how they make people feel. I also believe that He was instructing me to step up and speak out in order to help others. When my time comes to kneel before God on my judgement day, I may look back and say that I was not gifted enough to bring forth words that "shook" the world, but perhaps all of us can bring forth those special eight words that can help "shape and save" the world.

Scripture Passage:

Psalm 96:1-3 encourages us to do what?
How are you doing this in your own life?

Golden Nugget:

If you do not like something, resign yourself to its reality, accept it or require yourself to try to change it, but do not just complain. As Edmund Burke said, "All it takes for the forces of evil to triumph and rule the world is for enough good men to do nothing."

-36-

SAYINGS

The great philosopher Socrates allegedly said, "The unexamined life is not worth living." I agree. I also believe that the unlived life is not worth examining. There are people in all areas of life, some good and some bad. Some are known worldwide in politics, religion, commerce, music, art, sports, medicine, science, military, authors, explorers, investors, researchers, educators, etc. Books and movies chronicle their honors or horrors, and we cannot deny either their existence or their "footprints" on earth. Very often, I find that what I need to get through the day is not a book, a movie, a lecture, a conversation, a CD, a trip, a purchase, a thank you, or even a forgive me. What I find that I need is just a phrase or a saying that I can immediately grasp, hold onto, and "live with" for that day. Here are just some of the sayings that have helped me along the way.

> *Be careful with your words. Once they are said, they can be forgiven but not forgotten* (unknown).

This is the day the Lord has made let us rejoice and be glad (Psalm 118:24).

If things go wrong don't go with them (Unknown).

Silence is the best response to a fool (Unknown).

Don't compare your life with others, you have no idea what their journey is all about (Unknown).

Never leave until tomorrow what you can do today (Benjamin Franklin).

You don't have to attend every argument you are invited to (Unknown).

To be a Christian means to forgive the inexcusable because God forgave the inexcusable in you (C.S. Lewis).

No one can make you feel inferior without your consent (Unknown).

Enjoy the little things in life, for someday you will realize they were the big things (Unknown).

The greatest pleasure in life is achieving what people say you cannot do (Unknown).

You cannot start the next chapter of your life if you keep rereading the last one (Unknown).

Do one thing every day that scares you (Eleanor Roosevelt).

A Bible falling apart usually belongs to someone who isn't (Unknown).

Bible: Basic Information Before Leaving Earth (Unknown).

DFTBA: Don't Forget To Be Awesome (Unknown).

EIWP-GP: Everything Is Working Perfectly-God's Plan (Mary Etta Stoner Ph.D.).

The cause of most of man's unhappiness is sacrificing what he wants most for what he wants now (Gordon B. Hinckley).

You are capable of doing and becoming more than you realize (Unknown).

It always seems impossible until it's done (Nelson Mandela).

The right to do something does not mean doing it is right (William Safire).

Talent is God-given-Be humble.

Fame is man-given-Be grateful.

Conceit is self-given-Be careful. (John Wooden)

It's not the will to win that matters... Everyone has that. It's the will to prepare to win that matters (Coach Paul "Bear" Bryant).

I'm thankful to all those who said "no." It's because of them that I did it myself (Albert Einstein).

Start each day with a grateful heart (Unknown).

You can do anything but not everything (David Allen).

Don't ever mistake my silence for ignorance, my calmness for kindness, and my kindness for weakness (Unknown).

Whatever you are be a good one (Abraham Lincoln).

One thing is for certain, there will be one thing that will dominate your life. I strongly suggest it be something you can be proud of (Lou Holtz).

Life is not the way it's supposed to be. It's the way it is. The way we cope with it is what makes the difference (Virginia Satir).

To a man who once saw her cleaning the wounds of a leper and said, "I wouldn't do that for a million dollars," Mother Teresa replied, "neither would I."

An eye for an eye and the whole world would be blind (Mahatma Gandhi).

Sometimes you just need a good cry even if you don't know the reason you are crying (Unknown).

Words have worth and each one counts (Unknown).

I became acquainted with some of these sayings through travels, talking with people, and reading. I also became familiar with a good number of them because one of my beloved daughters-in-law, Jennifer, (who is a lawyer), has them prominently displayed in a room adjacent to her kitchen in New Bedford, Massachusetts. Thus, my second son, her husband, Dennis, as well as their five children, and other folks like this writer, can learn accordingly.

Scripture Passages:

Proverbs is a collection of wise sayings and good advice for daily living. There are thirty-one proverbs, one for each day of the month.

Read Proverbs 1.

What does it say about wisdom and understanding?

How do you go about attaining it?

Begin collecting your own wise sayings and refer to them often as you go through your daily life.

Golden Nugget:

If this is the best you can do in terms of style, substance, ethics, content, and reality, then be satisfied and be open to constructive criticism when it inevitably comes. At least, in the spirit of Teddy Roosevelt, you won't be numbered among those cold and timid souls who know neither victory nor defeat.

A FINAL GOLDEN NUGGET

As stated in the introduction, I have an interior driving force that compelled me to write this book. I do so as a Christian Catholic with belief in Jesus Christ as my Lord and Savior. I also do it with respect for all other religions as long as they do not force their beliefs upon others nor engage in extremism and/or terror as a means to an end.

I thank my immediate family: My wife, Monica, sons Patrick and Dennis, daughter Kristine, and their respective spouses, Sabrina, Jennifer, and Zack for their inexhaustible love and support. The same is true for our nine grandchildren: Briana, Savannah, McKenna, Matthew, Samuel, Elizabeth, Rachel, Michael, and Sophia. I also thank my countless friends who have supported and inspired me to keep going in all phases of my life.

A special thanks must be given to my granddaughter, Savannah, who is an undergraduate student at Appalachian State University in Boone, NC. It was Savannah who taught me the finer points of the keyboard so that thoughts could be transformed into words and eventually into this book. Acknowledgment is also given to my daughter-in-law, Jennifer Markey Golden, and her brother, John Markey, for their initial help and encouragement.

Prior to publication, I sought and received the opinions of a group of very talented people. Their comments and corrections were helpful beyond measure. I thank them deeply: Dr. Donald Burgo, Ms. Elizabeth Brennan, Ms. Patricia Etter, Dr. Francine Madrey, Dr. Helen McGlynn, Dr. Harrison Morson, Dr. Harriet Schwartz, and Dr. Robert Young.

Finally, enormous professional, inspirational, and editorial credit goes to, Dr. Larry Keefauver, Bestselling Author, and International Teacher. Larry was my Xulon Press partner and guide as I ventured into the land of professional authorship for the first time. His patience and wise counsel were inestimably important.

What I have shared here is, to the best of my knowledge, accurate. If evidence proves otherwise, it certainly was not intentional.

My final thought is if this book helps just one person on their pilgrim's journey, I rejoice!

-Denny Golden
Huntersville, North Carolina
For contact and book ordering: dcgolden95@gmail.com